Also by Dathan Belanger

The Faith of a Centurion

CLEAN FORGOTTEN PATRIOTS

IN THE AMERICAN WAR OF INDEPENDENCE

DATHAN BELANGER

CLAY BRIDGES
PRESS

Clean Forgotten Patriots
In the American War of Independence

Published by Clay Bridges in Houston, TX
www.claybridgespress.com

eISBN: 978-1-953300-52-2
ISBN: 978-1-953300-50-8 (paperback)
ISBN: 978-1-953300-51-5 (hardback)

TABLE OF CONTENTS

PREFACE

America presently finds itself in another rare, precarious moment. As a nation, we stand in the midst of a pivot point in our evolution. A dangerously progressive cancel culture movement (#cancelculture) has commenced among unpatriotic—and dare I say—Fascist elements and groups of our society, directly threatening peace and freedom; liberty and the American Republic as we know it. There are other terms for this: Communism, Marxism, Socialism. If you notice, they are all the dangerous forewarned "-isms" that have already wrought great damage in our world's history over time, and even led to some of our great wars, resulting in millions of deaths, ethnic cleansing (genocide), and mass suppression. These indoctrinating systems have never been successful . . . not anywhere, not once. Rather, they have been instrumental in creating mass unrest, overt rule by oppression, and Totalitarianism —another "-ism". Like typical Marxists and Communists, the organizers, doers, and instigators of this evil and unrest, deflect and blame their opposition for all they do; they demonstrate well-practiced, well-rehearsed deflection through propaganda and lies. This brings us full-circle to one of the main reasons I set out to write this book: To share the history and illuminate American progress. You see, if an uneducated, ignorant, and indoctrinated society were to suddenly succeed in 'canceling culture', we would lose our history.

We would lose our perspective, and we would lose our direction. Perhaps more importantly, we would lose that knowledge of 'from where we have come'.

History and all that is associated with it serve as our goal posts; our formative assessment of the lessons we have learned as a people, and as a nation, and where we must still go to become better. If culture is canceled . . . we lose sight of the goal posts, and we strip ourselves of meaning, along with most of the reasons for our very existence. Invented or unsubstantiated propaganda-driven terms that circulate through our insincere media channels have become prevalent and commonplace, and are dangerous. You can identify them when they are said in concert across multiple sources. They are terms right out of the Communist Marxist playbook, intended to divide a people – intended to divide us. These are terms that are most often based on race, health, and economy. Sound familiar? This propaganda serves no other purpose other than to sow and cede doubt, and also arrest confidence in the operations and history of a nation; to breed distrust, uprising, and fear, the latter of which has been one of the greatest mechanisms of control in modern memory. There is no other intent of the "-isms" and the propaganda that is born out of them, but to destroy a way of life, and to destroy our history. It is all manufactured, and only the patriotic people of the nation can defeat the movement, by holding the line, and standing strong.

I wrote this book so readers could experience a fascinating story and learn details of history they would not normally gain from a typical history book or academic text. I firmly believe in the value of historical fiction. These novels use fun stories to show how circumstances affected people personally, deeply, and emotionally, but also how our history directly contributed to our growth and betterment of society. Historical fiction not only tells us what happened, but it makes us feel; it elicits empathy for what our ancestors experienced in difficult times. Learning the truth of history is important, even if you don't like what you learn. Not all history is beautiful, but it does not mean it should be canceled. In fact, it takes great effort and courage to seek the truth and not be guided or influenced by negative emotions and prejudices. It is my hope that readers will come to understand a little more about the turning point in the American Revolution through the trials that took place at Valley Forge, the forgotten heroes that helped win the American Revolution and the groundswell of faith and prayer during the fight for a new nation.

Valley Forge took place between December 1771 and June 1778. The Rebel Army endured great suffering, choosing to stay and fight out of loyalty to the cause for independence, and to George Washington. The training and experience received by the soldiers resulted in the eventual birth of the American Army, which was subsequently a turning point in the war. After a harsh winter encampment, it was a 'ragtag', haphazardly assembled regiments from which emerged on the other side a well-trained army with a sense of pride and purpose, able to go against a seasoned nation's more established units of professional soldiers. In this book, you will soon meet historical characters that played integral roles during this particular time period, including George Washington, Baron Von Steuben, Alexander Hamilton, Marquis de Lafayette, Joseph Martin, and Mary McCauley - aka "Molly Pitcher".

In today's schools, most young Americans are taught an overly simplified version of the Revolutionary War. Many are educated that the war was decided only when rifles were grabbed from above fireplaces, with everyday middle-class colonial farmers marching off to fight the British. However, during the war colonists fought for liberty, while the Redcoats fought for taxes and King. There was much more meaning than often portrayed, and there was much more at stake, not unlike what is at stake should we lose our freedoms and liberties today – and contrary to what might be reported in our mostly disingenuous mainstream media, both are indeed being threatened and under attack as I write this. Many in our society and nation's schools overlook the numerous heroes that made this nation's Independence possible; that helped make it possible to feel a sense of safety in walking down streets or roads in our neighborhoods and towns. Yes, history has immeasurable value, and it sets my teeth on edge to see how much history has been forgotten, and now the modern attempts to have it canceled or erased. There are stories that need to be told so they do not fade away; so we may learn from our mistakes. So we may increase our tolerance and understanding, and appreciate our nation's forefathers, who put their lives on the proverbial line because they wanted a better, freer, more peaceful, and hopeful existence for themselves, their families, and the generations after them. This book will share the contributions made by Native Americans, African Americans, and mostly poor militia, who came from nothing. Yes, they fought together, side by side. There was not division in their collective resolve, but rather a unity in survival.

This nation should not forget the sacrifice of Native Americans, many of whom chose to support the Colonists at great risk because most clans favored the British. You will read the story of the Oneida Nation. It will explain why and how they chose to support the colonists. You will learn about the Oneida clan and meet historical Oneida characters, including Chief John Skenandoah, Jacob Reed, John Onondiyo, Polly Cooper, Daniel, and Thomas Shenendoah.

This nation also owes a great debt to African American patriots for filling the American ranks during the War for Independence. As George Washington himself admitted, they were essential to American Victory. It is estimated that up to 25% of the American Army at the final battle of Yorktown for American Independence was African American. In this book, you will meet the historical character Cato Bannister, an African American slave who chose to fight for American freedom, although he himself had none. This heart-wrenching and dedicated sacrifice can only be understood through the study of history, not its cancellation.

When the war began, many were willing to stop a musket ball for "liberty". There were a remarkable amount of ardent patriots. After a short time, colonists overwhelmingly relied on the poor, weary immigrants and vagabonds of society to take their place in the militia. Although Washington called the militia, "a broken staff," and consistently pressed the Continental Congress to authorize the recruitment of more able and stable troops, he knew there was no other choice but to tolerate what he had, despite feeling that the militiamen might harm the morale of the regulars; a concern that certainly had merit. However, regardless of Washington's reservations, the poor, courageous citizen-soldier of the militia was a contributing factor in the American victory.

Lastly, history today misses the value of faith and prayer during the time of the Revolution. Religion and prayer played a major role in the American Revolution by shaping thoughts and strengthening bonds. It also helped solidify trust among the soldiers and validated 'the fight', instilling hope in moments and hours when there seemed to be little. In the ensuing pages, you will acquire a better understanding of how faith and prayer unified the nation, resurrected morality among people, and fashioned appreciation for the practice of implementing good will among all. Our history is rich and decorated; humbling and tragic, but the lessons it teaches us hold virtues that are not often found on today's street corners, in today's protests, or even inside government hallways.

CONTINENTAL INTRODUCTION

The Revolution was at its most desperate time to stay alive. The British now controlled New York City and the strategic Fort Ticonderoga in upstate New York. In early September, Major General William Howe, commander of British forces in America, normally asleep at the job, was making his advance on Philadelphia. His mission was to capture the rebel capital and end the war. Howe loaded 15,000 British Regulars and Hessian troops on an armada of ships and sailed from New York City to the Chesapeake Bay in Maryland. His army next advanced north to capture Philadelphia. On September 11th General George Washington attempted to block Howe along the banks of the Brandywine River in Pennsylvania but was given a crushing defeat.

After the Battle of Brandywine Washington kept his army in Pennsylvania between Philadelphia and Reading to keep an eye on the British and to protect important military supplies recently moved out of the Philadelphia area to Reading. He gave orders to General Wayne, known as "Mad" Anthony Wayne with a modest force to harass the British at every chance. Wayne made a serious mistake of thinking his camp was well hidden. This would lead to a disaster.

September 20, 1777, at 10 PM, British troops attacked the camp under Major General Charles Grey. In silence Grey led the British charging into camp with fixed bayonets, to ensure total surprise on the unsuspecting Americans. In what became known as the Paoli

Massacre, Wayne's men fled in panic as the British poured into camp. Wayne's entire force was routed with, most of them captured.

Washington desperately wanted to prevent Howe from taking Philadelphia but a thousand of his men were barefoot and his army was exhausted from hard marches under heavy rains, fording rivers many times and often without food. On September 26, Philadelphia, America's largest city at the time, was captured by the British and Congress, which had been meeting there, fled. The number of delegates now present had dwindled to twenty from the fifty members who had signed the Declaration of Independence in 1776. Pennsylvanians lowered the Liberty Bell and carted it to the basement of the Zion Reformed Church in Allentown and hid it.

Washington made a run on the major British forces on October 4 at Germantown, when fresh reinforcements finally arrived. He inspired the amateur army to march 35 miles and fight a four-hour pitched battle. After some initial surprise and tough fighting, the Continental Army was forced to retreat and camp about 20 miles from Philadelphia. Washington dug in along the high hills of Whitemarsh for several weeks. In December, Howe tried to draw Washington from his strong defensive position, but the rebel army could not be dug and Howe was forced to withdraw back to Philadelphia.

The politicians in Congress with no understanding of military operations, now safely in York, Pennsylvania, urged Washington to take up the offensive and attack the British in Philadelphia, but the commander-in-chief was not an idiot. His men were exhausted and supplies were low. Many soldiers were already in tattered uniforms with some shoeless. He decided it was best to look for a location for the army's winter encampment. Washington sought the advice of his generals but they were unable to decide, finally, he decided the matter alone.

On December 12th, the army began the march to the west bank of the Schuylkill River at Valley Forge. It would be a miserable 13-mile march.

CHAPTER 1

PLOD ON

Hardness had already set in, of both body and elements. Every step forward on the frozen path was not without some degree of mental coercion. It had been like this for days, or perhaps months, having lost track of time. By dusk, the army of men had settled into a clearing, flanked by boulders and trees. They tried to relax by the fire while they waited for food, but relaxation in a time of war is an elusive luxury. According to government regulations, each soldier was to be issued a pound of flour and meat each day, along with a ration of beans or peas, and a pint of milk. However, on this day, 12,000 famished men would be fed "firecake", a dense mixture of flour and water hastily baked in the campfire. Weevils and maggots would frequently find their way into the flour store, and get cooked in the fire. Besides this protein-enriched edition, the cakes were flavorless and without much nutritional value.

The cold winter night quickly rolled in, and too tired for conversation, many of the men rested or dozed to the crackle of the campfire. Their beds were where they stood before sitting down. Shallow holes were dug out, hot coals tossed in, then covered again with dirt, on which the men hoped to warm their bodies. It was never enough. The bone-chilling cold was always a grim reminder of the horrors of war, and the yearning to return to the safety of loved ones; a longing for the very security of home that beckoned the fight to protect it and to secure it. This was in the mind of Samuel Fox, who shivered in the winter winds, his feet wrapped in bloodied strips of wool clothing that stained the snow, a substitute for his socks that had holes, and his shoes that had long ago eroded from the harsh plodding through winter's misery.

Samuel was far away from his family's farm in Rhode Island. Far away from his mother's delicious cooking and father's amusing stories. At home today Mother would probably be basting a fat turkey over a hot fire. Father's stories seemed to go on forever, but he would gladly trade the entertainment of watching snowfall for listening to one of Father's yarns. Each notch cut into the handle of his knife etched the memory of a friend he had lost in this war. There were many notches.

The morning brought a special treat, as the men were given a small piece of pork; the size of maybe two fingers. The pork was immediately soaked and warmed in the familiar cast iron pan they had used to make the fire cakes. Unless the pork was first soaked in water it would not be even slightly edible. Besides the copious amounts of salt, a large amount of fat was added. The meat resembled salted lard rather than a juicy piece of bacon. Nonetheless, to the hungry men it was a feast – and fuel for the day ahead.

After a quick camp clean-up, the men were on the march again. The snow was relentless. The wind howled, piling up snowdrifts from the storm that intensified and moved in overnight, making it difficult to see. Samuel was on the outside of the column walking bent over against the cold, protecting his eyes with his arms. The surrounding forest looked blurry in his vision, then vanished, consumed in white. With a thud, Samuel smacked hard into a horse. The crash was enough to make him lose his balance. He dropped his musket and smacked the ground face first in the cold snow. The surrounding men in the column immediately broke formation to help. The man on horseback stopped and jumped off to assist. An embarrassed and confused Samuel was quickly rolled over onto the cold snow and examined. The man on horseback was none other than General George Washington. Even with the snowfall, there was no escaping the sight of his signature Roman-shaped nose, the crease in his chin, and high forehead. "We're all having a bit of trouble seeing where we are going?" Washington pointed to his horse. "Would you like to sit on my horse, "Blueskin", for a while?" Samuel looked at the striking gray horse rumored to be given to Washington by a sultan in Morocco. Samuel would have liked nothing more than to ride that horse. He swallowed hard.

"I'm fine, but thank you for the offer, sir." Washington patted Samuel on the back then mounted his horse and moved forward with the column.

Unsteadily, Samuel pushed himself to his feet. He brushed off the snow as best he could from his tattered uniform, wool overcoat, and achy limbs, grabbed his musket, and rejoined the march. His pride was more hurt than the bruises he felt. The slow-moving column of men trudged forward, a sea of mismatched Continental uniforms. With each painful step in the driving snow, they were closer to Valley Forge, where a trove of much-needed supplies awaited them. Every frozen face was grim against the frigid wind, and on every mind were thoughts of warm winter quarters.

"Sammy", as his mother would endearingly call him whenever she touched his strong chin, was grateful for his long brown hair because it covered his ears and the back of his neck. He also had heard a rumor that the Native Americans believed long hair contributed to inner wisdom and sharper senses; an antenna for greater intuition. He lowered his head, and his tricorn hat, to combat the elements, and like a battle cry, he charged forth with the rest of his comrades. The hat had become a keepsake, worn by his friend Benjamin Tucker, who died at the Battle of Paoli on September 20. For Samuel, the hat had become Benjamin – when he removed it at the end of a long day and placed it beside him; when he ran his fingers along the woolen brim and recalled Benjamin's last words, "And 'neath the dirt I will lay my head. O! tell my mother the revolution is worth dying for, her wayward son goes to Jesus in heaven." In times like these, when he lowered it against the odds, he was again reminded of Benjamin.

The Continental infantry was equipped similarly to British soldiers. Along with his 10 lb musket that grew heavy after a while, he carried on his right side a leather cartridge box that held thirty rounds of ammunition, a supply of flints, and a musket cleaning tool. On his left side attached with linen shoulder straps, he carried his wooden canteen and a socket bayonet in a leather scabbard. Across his right shoulder he had a haversack, made of linen, to carry his food rations, and his horn-handled eating utensils, along with a tin cup and plate. The haversack was empty. A knapsack held his personal items including, a comb, a razor for shaving, a tinderbox with steel for starting a fire, and a hook with some twine so that he could catch fish when the army was near water. Around his neck was a lead cross given to him by his mother. He was told the simple cross had been passed down in the family for many generations. The original owner was thought to be a Templar knight.

Samuel was a budding, young man naive to the world outside his family's small farm. As a child, he longed for an adventure. His copy of Don Quixote was well-worn with pages falling out. One of the first to join the Continental army, now 21, he was disheartened from the effects of the losing war. He now understood he was not a character in a book assured his adventure would lead to a happy ending. This adventure likely would lead to his death.

Samuel was empty of putting notches on his knife. The most recent notch came just prior to the march for winter camp. The British under Sir William Howe left a small garrison at Philadelphia then settled at nearby Germantown with the bulk of their force near Valley Forge. Washington, under heavy fog and darkness on

October 3, tried to replicate his luck at the Battle of Trenton where he was successful in defeating Hessian mercenaries in a surprise attack. Washington pressed the attack, determined to destroy the British at camp. Samuel and his friend Johnathan were in a column of regular troops led by General John Sullivan. Sullivan had a chip on his shoulder to prove after his failure and defeat at Brandywine. At the onset, Sullivan's forces were routing the British. However, when they became low on ammunition and heard the thunder of cannons, they were forced to withdraw and retreat. Johnathan took a musket ball in the back of his head. He never saw it coming. Samuel had only time to say a quick prayer for his friend with musket rounds whistling everywhere. He was left on the battlefield and became a memory notch in the handle of his knife.

The campfire flames flickered and created red sparks that danced in the breeze.

"You here!" shouted a voice, snapping Samuel from his thoughts, "the British are taken to callen us "buckshot" now," Ethan Clark said, taking up a spot beside Samuel on the path. Ethan was of similar age, dark black hair with a coat and uniform much like Samuel's, but he had no cap. He wore strips of cloth around his head to keep warm.

Samuel chuckled, "Better to be called a "buckshot" than "Yankee Peas" which they've been calling us of late," he said.

Ethan smiled. "Those Brits deserve a little buckshot with a musket ball." He paused for a moment then his face suddenly grew serious. "Sorry to hear about Johnathan, I knew you two were close."

Samuel was silent, unable to speak. Memories flashed through his mind. Ethan patted Samuel on the shoulder and changed the subject.

"I can't wait to get to Valley Forge, warm lodging and some good food," said Ethan.

"I hope so," said Samuel, "this march has been miserable. It would be great to be able to wear a pair of shoes again. There must be plenty in supply at Valley Forge."

Ethan frowned. "Another day of fire cake and Methinks I shall go mad. I crave juicy meat and fresh bread to sink my teeth into."

"Allow us to change the subject and not talk about food," said Samuel.

"I imagine that's a good thought. Samuel, doth you have a wench you're courting back home."

"Nah, not yet my brother is the one with the way with girls. I fancy at some point I'll begin my search." Samuel grinned.

"My sweetie, Abigail. She's the prettiest wench you'll ever see. Her parents' God bless hast taken a liking to me. Wherein the wars over I'll go back to being a clerk. Not much as far as wages yet enough to get by. What job do you aim for when you get back?"

"Ain't granted that much thought, to be honest. I do love workin' towards the farm. Somethin' about the dirt on my hands. I know not how to describe it. Hard work yet peaceful at the like time," said Samuel.

"Well all will deserve a slice of peace when this war is done I reckon. We get through this war we've earned it."

The campfire continued to fight back the cold but did nothing to absorb the men's worries.

The men crossed the Schuylkill River on a rickety bridge in an area called "the Gulph". The snowstorm was followed by days of icy rain that forced the men to camp there until the roads were made passable. On December 18th, the soaked and miserable troops observed a Day of Thanksgiving declared by Congress for the American victory in October, at Saratoga, New York, in which Benedict Arnold, one of Washington's best infantry commanders, ignoring orders from his commander Gates to remain in his quarters, led an attack that forced the British to retreat to Saratoga. Ten days later, it resulted in the surrender of the once over-confident British General Burgoyne. A Continental soldier named Joseph Plumb Martin succinctly recalled that Thanksgiving feast years later as a "½ cup of rice and a tablespoon of vinegar!"

CHAPTER 2

MISERY LOVES COMPANY

The sun climbed to its zenith and the forest gave way abruptly. Fewer than several hundred paces of cleared ground separated trees from Valley Forge. The wind howled with fury six days before Christmas, the weary and hungry men arrived, but there would be no celebrating nor a holiday feast. The needed supplies were not there. No food, no equipment, only the cold to greet them. They were entering into a nightmare, an ice-cold one.

Ragged men exhausted at arrival did not have much time for their dark thoughts. There was a lot of labor that needed to be done quickly. Officers immediately barked out orders for the camp construction. It was too cold for tents, so the arriving troops began constructing the approximately 1,700 primitive log huts in lines to form streets. Each would have a stone fireplace and a roof of the board, straw, or canvas. The huts were hastily built into the ground about two-feet below with a dirt floor and most doors consisted of no more than a cloth covering. To encourage speed, Washington himself offered one dollar to every party of twelve in each regiment that completed quality work the fastest. The conditions they would live in this winter would be similar to living in dungeons. The cells would be cramped, drafty, damp, and smell awful. Valley Forge received its name from the iron forge that was constructed along Valley Creek in the 1740s. It contained a burned-out sawmill and gristmill and once held a cache of American military stores, but a raid on September 18th by Hessian General Wilhelm von Knyphausen on behalf of Britain pillaged the supply magazine at Valley Forge. The Hessians captured some supplies, destroyed others, and burned the forges along with other buildings—despite the best efforts of Lieutenant Colonel Alexander Hamilton and Captain Henry "Light-Horse Harry" Lee to evacuate what supplies they could escape with.

Why did Washington choose this site for winter camp with so little in supply? Mainly because its high terrain made it easy to defend. Any attackers would have to charge uphill. In addition, it was close enough to Philadelphia to monitor the actions of the British troops sheltered there, yet far enough away to prevent a surprise attack on the Continental Army.

The total number of soldiers sheltered at Valley Forge would be 12,000 men, along with 400 Regimental Camp Followers, women, and children. Most of the women were wives or family members of the soldiers. They were paid primarily in the form of rations in exchange for washing the army's laundry, sewing and mending garments, cooking food, and tending the sick and wounded. Washington understood that a soldier could die quickly from the disease if his uniform was dirty and threadbare, but also understood that emotional support to a soldier could be equally as important.

Building the huts for the army was fairly simple. Finding supplies and feeding the troops would be a daunting challenge. Approximately 1 in 5 soldiers had no footwear and food was about to run out. The supplies were out there but getting them to Valley Forge would be the challenge. Transportation to Valley Forge was a major stumbling block; no suitable roads connected Valley Forge to civilization. Also, there was no trust in the nearly worthless

Continental money. Often farmers would hide their supplies rather than take the Continental money. The man in charge of this supply mess was the Quartermaster General, Thomas Mifflin. Mifflin was a born politician and a wealthy Philadelphia merchant who wanted glory on the battlefield not the boredom of moving equipment and supplies. He literally ignored the job.

Samuel swung a pickaxe and lodged it into the cold and rocky New England soil with a sharp thwack! His face was red from the bitter wind stinging his face. He was by this time shivering and damp, not to mention hungry. Rain began to fall slowly at first in cold droplets then turned into a steady rain. The smell of the moist dirt emerged strongly over the rain-washed ground. The thick brown mud was not cold enough to freeze yet clung to his feet, sapping what little heat his body produced. Icy brown water soaked into his socks, soddening his feet. In a wide arc, he swung the pickaxe again. Thwack! His back ached as he continued to swing and strike, swing and strike. The rain stopped but Samuel was already soaked to the bone, miserable as a cat tossed in a bucket of cold water. Like many soldiers he could not escape the thought, what the hell am I doing here. He plodded away, working until the sun grew dim.

Samuel made his way to his cabin.

"If you would have my pardon, soldier. I never got your name in our introduction."

Samuel's eyes grew large. "Yes, Sir, General Washington. My name is Samuel Fox."

"A very strong last name. A fox is known as sly, but it is a resourceful and noble creature," said Washington. "I'm sure Valley Forge has come as a surprise with its lack of supplies." Washington looked down at Samuel's dirty foot wrappings, his only protection from the elements.

Samuel fought back a frown. "Valley Forge isn't exactly paradise, General, but we will make do. Will take it to the Brits in the spring and won't be needing a winter camp next year."

"I applaud thy enthusiasm, Samuel. A question for you. I receive reports from my officers frequently. I'd rather say they may be counted on as yes men. Can I rely on you to set the records straight?"

Samuel's eyes gleamed with pride. "Yes, General, I'll be straight with you. As straight as a musket ball i' the hands of a trained sharpshooter. Mark my words."

Washington nodded. "Consider 'em marked. Wot what you can. Wot what you can. There is no bawbling detail that is not important. Learn to read 'twixt the lines what your eyes do not see 'twixt the lines. An ancient Greek poet named Archilochus wrote a parable many years since with the following moral: 'The fox knows many things, yet the hedgehog knows one big thing.' Basically, the meaning of this is that some people see the details i' all's they do, like the fox, while others are great at having one singular vision, like the hedgehog. I hast enough hedgehogs. Be my fox, Samuel. Be my fox. Take care of yourself I shall surely bid upon you in due haste."

Samuel was given quarters in an already constructed cabin to be shared with eleven other weary men. The cramped space had wooden bunks built into the sides of the cabin with a thin layer of straw to lay on. A fire, the only light in the cabin, was burning brightly in the stone fireplace. He quickly took off his soaked foot wrappings and placed them near the fireplace to dry. He took off his socks, rang the water out on the dirt floor near the fireplace, and sat with his swollen and wrinkled feet as close to the fire as he could get without burning.

"Samuel, good to see you. Looks like we're gonna share this dark dungeon together." Ethan spoke lightly. "You hungry? No rations were given out after this morning but I've been saving this." From his coat, Ethan pulled out a small pumpkin. "Be glad to share it with you." Ethan placed a small flat stone in the fireplace then cut the pumpkin in half. From his haversack, he pulled out two tiny hollowed-out gourds, each with a small cork stopper. Removing the corks, he sprinkled some cinnamon and black pepper onto the pumpkin. He placed the pumpkin halves on the stone in the fireplace, each half on its thick, skin side, and roasted them. The aroma of pumpkin drifted everywhere. Many a wishful eye looked upon Samuel and Ethan in earnest as they watched the two eat.

The sound of a door-knocking was barely heard in the noisy cabin. The tall knocker walked in, nearly hitting his head on the short ceiling. The site of George Washington received their attention quickly. The men knocked themselves about to stand up quickly. Washington motioned them to be seated. "Lads, I appreciate your sacrifice in this here cause of liberty. Your sacrifice is great but let me assure you that the reward of freedom is worth fighting for." He cleared his throat. "Allow us to rouse and help each other, and learn all of the orbs that a freeborn, searching for liberty on his land, is superior to any foreign invader. The harder the conflict, the greater the triumph." He pulled from under his coat a set of worn leather shoes with remarkably no holes. He spotted Samuel and handed them to him with a warm smile. "You may walk better with these." Samuel stood up to receive his gift. His head felt light, knees weak as he held the precious shoes in disbelief.

Samuel stuttered, "Thu-Thank you, General."

Washington sighed. "Just wish I had more to offer." He then shook the hands of every man, thanking them individually for their service. Into the dark night, he departed. The men talked for a while after the visit but finally, weariness and a dwindling fire brought the conversation to a close. One by one the men drifted off to sleep.

In a dream, the sun's warm rays stretched over the gentle bay in Newport, Rhode Island. Two brothers were raking for the hard shell clams called Quahogs. Well, they should have been. One boy named Duncan laughed out, "You know she likes you." Samuel grabbed a fist full of mud and launched it at Duncan, missing widely. Duncan snickered uncontrollably. Samuel came closer, ready to smack a pile of mud on top of Duncan's head. Duncan escaped with a quick dive.

"Boys, knock it off!" a man's loud voice bellowed from the shore. It was their father. "Your mother has been calling you for dinner.

Now fetch yourselves quickly or it will be trouble for you." The boys immediately stopped their antics and brought out the basket that should have been filled with Quahogs. They dashed home, soaked and filthy from the mud.

Once home, they washed up, dressed quickly, and ran to the table. Laid out on a long oak table was a banquet. Samuel's mouth watered at the sight of the food. There was his favorite delicacy, roasted pheasant. The table also held a mix of roasted vegetables, beans, and fresh bread. A pitcher of fresh spruce beer completed the show. Samuel sat down and a bowl of potatoes popped into existence. He greedily reached for one. "Wake up, Samuel." A nudge to his ribs made Samuel jerk awake to see a soldier he recognized as Jethro, a sharp-faced man, holding a candle. "Guard duty," Jethro whispered. "Be quick about it, I want to get back to bed. The bid of duty is the ability to do another." In the blackness of the cabin, Samuel brushed off the straw from his coat, which he was using as a blanket. Putting on his coat, he then grabbed his musket and leather ammunition box from under his bunk. Before departing, Samuel threw some wood into the glowing red embers of the fireplace. Jethro used his candle to guide him outside of the cabin then disappeared in a hurry.

Under moonlight much brighter than the darkness of the cabin, Samuel walked slowly to his guard post in the cold trenches. He took his position with only the stars to keep him company. The white orbs fought to hold back the darkness.

ONEIDA INTRODUCTION

A new day began with the sun rising over the homeland of the Oneida Nation. Their lands had been owned for generations. Well, not really owned. The Oneida people would be one of the first to admit that no one truly owns the land. The land belongs to mother earth, and the earth is a blessing given by God. In his infinite wisdom, God had a plan for the Oneida. The Revolutionary War would be a pivotal moment for the Oneida.

Onyota'a:ka, which means "People of the Standing Stone," is the Oneida people's name for themselves; it is converted from the English articulation as Oneida. In an ancient legend of their people, an enemy tribe pursued them into a woodland clearing, when the Oneida suddenly vanished. It was surmised that the Oneida shapeshifted into stones found in a clearing. Thus the people took to calling themselves "People of the Standing Stone".

The Oneida tribe, made up of several villages, was part of the Haudenosaunee Confederacy, meaning "People of the Longhouse." The British called the Confederacy the League of Five Nations and the French called them the Iroquois Confederacy. Prophet and great Peacemaker Deganawida with his disciple commonly known as Hiawatha founded the confederacy after years of blood feuds. This Confederacy was one of the first and longest-lasting democracies in the world. A peaceful society that existed over 500 years until Europeans arrived to undermine the natives and pit tribes against one another, for the sake of greed. The introduction of firearms and European diseases such as influenza, measles, and smallpox led to thousands of deaths.

The original Confederacy started with five tribes, the Oneida, Mohawks, Senecas, Cayugas, and Onondagas; a sixth, the Tuscaroras, was added as a non-voting member fleeing British Colonial expansion in 1722. The Confederacy did not choose sides at the beginning of the Revolution. This allowed the Confederacy to take advantage of both sides during the war because at any time they could join a side if provoked. Neutrality quickly crumbled and the drum beats of war sounded. Most of the Cayugas, Mohawks, Onondagas, and Senecas sided with the British and Loyalists in order to preserve their culture and stop the encroachment upon their lands. The Oneida, joined by the Tuscaroras, chose the colonists' side because of their close proximity and connections with Christian communities. It is important to know that although leaders of the tribe had taken the rebel side, not every Oneida agreed with the alliance. A minority of the Oneida did choose to support the British.

The Oneida shed blood for the colonists' cause at "A Place of Great Sadness," the Battle of Oriskany on August 6, 1777. This battle was one of the bloodiest clashes in the Revolutionary War. Several Confederacy allies and a party of Loyalists ambushed a Rebel military force with allied Oneidas that was trying to relieve the siege of Fort Stanwix, known today as Fort Schuyler. It was brother against brother that resulted in upfront and personal hand-to-hand combat against each other. The Great law, given by the Peacemaker, that enjoined the Confederacy from taking arms against each other was broken, and as a result, it shattered the moral and spiritual footing of the great Confederacy.

CHAPTER 3

NOT JUST FUN AND GAMES

It was a sunlit day in early spring, and the sky a cloudless, soft blue. The air was cool but not cold. Jacob Reed, also called Aksiaktatye, stood, holding his lacrosse stick breathing heavily. As perspiration slowly dripped down from his face, he prepared to receive the ball, the intensity in his eyes evident. He was determined to win the game. His lean muscles built from hard labor and a good diet flexed as he prepared himself to move in an instant. Medicine men acting as coaches looked upon the players with anxiety and excitation. The gathered crowd was jubilant, routing for their respective teams to win.

The deerskin ball was tossed quickly to Jacob. He moved his stick close to his chest. His eyes stared at the pole about a hundred feet in front of him. The score was tied, the first to reach twenty points would win. Daniel and Thomas, the tribal chief Shenendoah's sons, rushed in front of Jacob to block for him. The brothers' appearance was almost identical. They seemed to always carry a smile that radiated energy and fun. In a crash, the blockers were struck head-on by a large pack of defenders charging. The result was a pile of players on the ground. Jacob leaped for his life over the mass of bodies and continued his chase for the scoring pole. He stopped and spun, barely missing a desperate defender. But he did feel the defender's stick slap his shoulder hard. Ignoring the pain, he stood up to shoot. Suddenly, he was blindsided by a hard hit. He crumpled to the ground. The ball dropped out of the basket from his stick and was scooped up by the attacker John, also called Onondiyo, a sachem or chief from the Turtle Clan.

John was head and shoulders taller than any of the players. He was an Adonis among the tribe. His face was strong and defined, his features molded from stone. His long dark hair was held by a leather cord around his temples. Jacob was stunned and dazed but quite aware of the hoots and howls from Turtle Clan telling him that the opposing team had just scored the win. Jacob remained on the ground catching his breath feeling disappointed.

"Good game," John stood over him with his hand outstretched. Jacob took the hand and was lifted up. John smiled "It looks like Wolf Clan hosts the camaraderie feast."

Jacob grimaced. "You hit hard, my friend." He rubbed his shoulder. "Well, at least the Turtle Clan finally won a game. I was starting to think…" Jacob's grimace turned into a smirk. The two men looked at each other, laughed, then they briefly embraced. "Ouch, my shoulder!" overemphasized Jacob.

"You will be fine," John said. "Hard work and pain help lead us to a pure heart."

Jacob harrumphed. "What are you going to say to me next? That which does not dispatch us makes us stronger?"

"I would have mentioned this, but I think a Wolf Clan warrior such as yourself already knows this," said John.

Jacob tied his long black hair behind his back, and in doing so uncovered his dark brown eyes and a noble face that showed confidence beyond his years. John and Jacob, weary and hungry, traveled together towards Kanonwalohale.

Lacrosse, sometimes called the "Little Brother of War" because it was often played to settle disputes between villages or tribes, helped keep the peace among the Haudenosaunee Confederacy. Today the game was played to simply please the Creator. The lacrosse players, coaches, and a large crowd headed to Kanonwalohale, also the home of Jacob, to feast and celebrate the win of the Turtle Clan.

Kanonwalohale, located in the Colony of New York, was established after the Oneida suffered savage raids from the French colony of Quebec, which was trying to control their fur trade. In 1615, Samuel de Champlain and Huron Native Americans attempted to destroy the Oneida. The Oneidas managed to ward off the attack, but they were forced to abandon their settlement and moved a few miles westward. This new settlement, called Kanonwalohale, was also called the castle because the dwellings and valuable storage structures were surrounded by tall wooden palisades, with a moat bordering this. It protected the Oneida, which included Wolf Clan, Bear Clan, and Turtle Clan.

Translated from the Oneida language, Kanonwalohale means "Enemy's Head on a Pole," in reference to an enemy warrior's skull displayed. The village that held one-third of the Oneida population closely resembled its founders' links to Europeans. No longer did the Oneidas live in longhouses with fellow members of their extended family. Family continued to be important, but the desire for more material comforts persuaded the Kanonwalohale to disperse themselves in separate houses without their extended family. More than sixty homes were constructed, some constructed with traditional bark and others with European-style wood frames, and a few log cabins.

Kanonwalohale was very agrarian; it combined European and Oneida practices, and European animals. The populous used oxen to cultivate with plows and many households kept a dairy cow for milk. They also raised turkeys, chickens, and hogs for sources of meat and even sheep for wool. Kanonwalohale was indistinguishable from any Colonial settlement.

Food was already being prepared for the feast; both clans readied food in the event their team lost. Those of the winning team also were free to bring dishes. The players and coaches mixed with the other team in a wide circle then they sat down on a field of plush grass. Most of the Oneida tribe gathered around the players. Many in the crowd were still hallooing and yelping. A quick silence came when the food began to be served.

A tired, muscle-ached, and hungry Jacob was enjoying his meal sitting next to John, the star player of the game. John looked like an arrow in a drawn bow. John motioned he wanted to talk but Jacob shook his head. Jacob was too busy stuffing himself with large amounts of corn, beans, and squash and did not want his meal to be disturbed. After he was satisfied and after a loud burp, he turned to John. "Aaah . . . My hunger is tamed and I give thanks to the Lord for the food we have. What is it you would like to discuss, my friend?" Jacob changed his language to English. "I know you are practicing hard upon't. Let us converse in the tongue of the English."

John exhaled, ran his hands through his hair, and looked around sullenly. John was practicing his English but was not as good at it as Jacob, who could both read and write it. "What do you think chief Shenandoah and the clan ma—" Short pause. "—mothers will decide at the conference?" said John.

An Oneida delegation was meeting with General George Washington's good friend Marie Joseph Paul Yves Roch Gilbert du Motier, marquis de Lafayette, known simply as Lafayette, and representatives at a conference to the east a few miles away in Johnstown, New York, to discuss the British threat. Washington was known by the Oneida as a hero in the French and Indian War. A hero that through some divine Providence never so much as received a scratch from a bullet despite his size. Horses were killed beneath him, his hat was shot off his head but never a scar. It was rumored an unknown Native American Chief prophesied that "Washington would become a chief among chiefs, and a people yet unborn, shall hail him as the father of a mighty empire!" Washington desperately wanted the Oneida and Tuscarora warriors to join his army at Valley Forge. These Native Americans could discourage attempts of desertions from the Continental Army, help capture enemy soldiers, gain vital intel as scouts, and counter the British raids in the area messing with supplies and harassing the colonists. The conference was vital to the Colonists to gain allies for so many tribes supported the British.

The Oneida delegation sent the Oneida War Chief John Skenandoah, known as Oskanondonha, also known as "The Deer." He was a War Chief, a position chosen on ability and merit, not descent. The delegation also included a council of women elders. Although the chief of a clan may hold the power of military decision and trade arrangements, he could be removed at any time by a council of women elders of that clan. The goal of the delegation was to support the Colonists without causing too much harm to themselves. Above all, they would put the needs of preserving the Oneida Nation first.

John continued his conversation with Jacob although he switched back to his native tongue. "Of what I heard, George Washington is begging for scouts to use against the British and his men are desperate for food supplies. The Confederacy is split, we have chosen to support the Colonists. We need to move now and give aid while it can still make a difference! What will the British do to us if the Colonists are defeated? I reason not fine, indeed for our survival."

Jacob frowned. "You know I wanted peace. I went with a delegation to Caughnawaga to plead with the Mohawks in September of 1775 to maintain their neutrality with the Confederacy. But after visiting with Continental General Philip Schuyler in June 1776, in Albany, New York, I was struck with the number of troops and the colonists resolved to fight it out with Britain. I knew sides would be taken and the Confederacy would shatter and take sides. Let us wait till Chief Shenendoah returns and addresses us. The more you ask how far we need to go, the longer the journey will seem."

A perfect distraction began with the beating of drums. The music pulled at their hearts with every beat. Jacob and John rushed to the music and joined the gathering dancers. Shortly the drumbeat changed and the dancing began. Chants were added to the heartbeat of the drumming; this was the Round dance, also called Circle or Friendship dance. The dancers moved in a circular pattern in a clockwise direction, stepping and swinging arms to the hard and soft beat. Daniel, who blocked for Jacob earlier in today's lacrosse game, led the dancers to coil up like a snake and then uncoil. As the dancers passed in front of one another, they exchanged greetings, joy, and laughter.

Jacob lost his footing and slipped, accidentally sticking his foot out just enough for Polly Cooper to catch it and fall hard. There was a momentary flare of anger in Polly's face that went away just as quickly. The young woman quickly picked herself up, her head whipped around hard, and she stared at Jacob. She was dressed in a long skirt that was decorated with beautiful beads and dyed purple porcupine quills. Her eyes were a deep, earthy brown, the color of rich soil after pouring rain. She was fine to look and radiated an intelligent beauty. Even though she wore two braids instead of one braid, signifying she was not married, she walked with the confidence of someone a decade older. "I'm not a lacrosse player, Jacob, to be knocked into," she blurted out. "Do you have the agility of a wolf or that of a kicking Jack?" All the words were in the native tongue except for the last word in English. She tried to maintain a smooth face, but the beginnings of a grin made her cheeks seem even plumper. To avoid laughing she jumped back into the dance. Jacob stood still for a second, trying to remember what the word Jack meant in English, then found his way back into the dance. He failed to decipher the meaning.

When the drums silenced and dancers began to leave, Jacob found Polly to ask her what a Jack was. Mixing with Polly was like wading the streams. However peaceful the water looked, the currents beneath could snatch you off your feet. Polly stared at him with those deep pools in her eyes and explained. "It's the nickname for a male donkey. You were acting like one earlier." She began to pace back and forth. Abruptly she frowned and stopped pacing. "I overheard you talking with John about the Confederacy breaking up. You men are stubborn like a Jack." She bit her lower lip in frustration. "Mothers carry a child from birth. Mothers nurse and care for a child in every way so that the infant knows the hands that hold them are a dependable love. All men, no matter what country they are fighting for, they all have mothers, and mothers don't send their sons out to kill other mothers' sons. The peace in the Confederacy was secured at Onondaga Lake, where they planted a Tree of Peace and proclaimed the Laws of the Confederacy. Peace needs to be kept. In every decision, we must consider the impact of our decisions on the next generation." Her shoulders slumped and her voice faltered. "The great Peacemaker said we should all love one another and live together in peace. If we fail him, it will only lead to disaster."

Jacob did not know what to say. He knew it was too late for the Confederacy to heal. "I agree with you, Polly, we are headed for disaster." Polly nodded in agreement and walked away. It was getting late; the stars came out to play and the evening took on the scent of the night. Tonight at least there was peace, but it would not last for long. The winds of change were coming to displace everything.

CHAPTER 4

LOVE OF KANONWALOHALE

The early morning sunlight stretched over Kanonwalohale, embracing it. The springy aroma added to the morning mist; a rich, damp vegetative odor, the wet soil of winter drying up, combined with the sweet fragrance of flowers. Both men and women were up early to work their small farms outside the fortified walls. Traditionally, Oneida men were in charge of hunting, trading, along with war, and Oneida women were in charge of farming, property, and family. Many men now joined the women at their European-style homes, working the field, and caring for livestock.

Jacob stretched his arms, waking with the first rays of morning light touching him. He winced, feeling the aches of yesterday's lacrosse game. He knew for sure there would be a large bruise on his shoulder from the stick that hit him at the game. Removing his blankets, he shifted off his bed's husk mattress, then quickly dressed. Jacob was proud of his small European framed clapboard home. Although some residents of Kanonwalohale were living in large and better-built houses, he was content. Instead of a community in which all was shared or all went without, Kanonwalohale had started representing a world of haves and have nots. No European furniture or any furniture graced his home with the exception of a trunk that held his prized goods. He moved slowly due to his sore muscles that fought any cooperation. He went to the trunk and pulled out a good-sized copper pan leaning against a large brass pot. Walking over to his fireplace, he threw a bunch of small sticks that quickly lit in the embers still warm from last night. When the flames flickered then died down a bit, he pulled out a good portion of warm embers and placed his copper pan on them, making a breakfast of cornmeal cakes with a good portion of roasted squash. After finishing breakfast, he dressed. He put on a cotton shirt, dyed a light blue, then put on his short breechcloth, or loincloth, with a beautifully decorated apron panel attached in front and behind; next was his soft, leather leggings and moccasins. Jacob lost track of time. Oh, Dilberries! I don't want to be late for church. Moving quickly, he rushed out the door to attend the morning prayer service officiated by Good Peter.

Agwalongdong was "Breaking of the Twigs" and also called "Good Peter." Peter was a Warrior from the Bear Clan, who recently left the village of Oquaga due to disagreements of faith. He was a devout Christian, converted in 1748 and he began eloquently preaching at Oquaga in the summer of 1753. He had a gift of incorporating traditional Oneida ideas and values into his Christian teachings so the people could understand his message.

The warrior founders of Kanonwalohale, sometimes called New Oneida, had begun to drift away from time-honored Iroquois religious beliefs. A majority of Kanonwalohale were Christian, with only a few not accepting the new faith. The largest conversion took place with the arrival of young missionary Samuel Kirkland, a native of Connecticut. Kirkland offered the warriors an alternative set of beliefs that also functioned to uphold many essential Oneida cultural constructions without disturbing the authority of the sachems and matrons. Many Oneida were baptized as Christians in the decade before the colonists' revolution began. Kirkland worked to help them with education and with struggles with alcohol. Through relations with him, many Oneida began to form stronger links to the colonists. They began to think of the colonists as their fellow Christian brothers and subsequently felt bound to help them against Britain.

Jacob navigated around the many farms of Kanonwaloale to arrive at the small log cabin church near the center of town, framed with glass windows. He sat on the crowded floor next to chief Shenendoah's two children, Daniel and Thomas, with about thirty others, both men and women, who were facing Peter who had already begun preaching. He was fired up, talking in a powerful, booming voice. "My friends, we must continue to have fellowship and love as Christian brothers. The Great Peacemaker who was sent from God the creator brought the confederacy many years of peace through the power of love." He pointed at the crowd sitting before him. "In John 13, Jesus commands us to love one another. A new commandment I give to you, that you love one another, even as I have loved you, that you also love one another." Peter's voice softened; putting his hands together, he touched his fingers gently and continued, "In Mathew 22 when Jesus was asked by his disciples what commandments must be kept above all, Jesus said unto them, Thou shalt love the Lord thy God with all thy heart, and with all thy soul, and with all thy mind. This is the first and great commandment. And the second is like, unto it, Thou shalt love thy neighbor as thyself. On these two commandments hang all the law and the prophets." Pausing in thought, the sadness of the Confederacy split flowed through Peter's veins. His bottom lip quivered ever so slightly and his eyes held back a tear. With great emotion in his voice, he continued, "Samuel Kirkland deems it righteous to support the colonists against the British and I agree. We will not fail our fellow neighbors and brothers in their time of need." He exhaled a long breath. "Now go in peace and may God be with you."

The group rose quickly, but many lingered to talk and enjoy fellowship. Daniel slapped Jacob's shoulder, fortunately not the bruised one. "Good game, Jacob, we almost had them." Jacob smiled. In a flash, Thomas slapped his other shoulder. The bruised one. Jacob drew back with a scowl.

"Sorry about that . . . forgot. Hey, good job tripping Polly last night!" said Thomas.

Jacob scanned the crowd quickly but did not see Polly. His scowl turned into a grin. "It was an accident," Jacob pleaded.

Thomas and Daniel began to laugh till their ribs hurt. "Well, you better watch your back," Thomas chuckled. "She has the spirit of a warrior in her."

Jacob's voice took on a mock sternness. "I will take that under advisement, Thomas."

Peter appeared abruptly. "I could hear you men laughing above all the talking in here. What is so amusing?"

Jacob explained the accidental trip at the dance.

"She has the spirit of a warrior, but she knows the greatest strength is gentleness," beamed Peter. "Polly will make a great clan mother one day."

The men nodded their approval. Peter shook their hands and went back into the crowd.

The crowd began to shrink to only a handful. Thomas turned to Jacob in an attempt of seriousness. It was difficult for Thomas or his brother to take anything seriously. "Soon we will be at war. I feel it coming. My blood tingles with anticipation."

"Time to sharpen our tomahawks," Daniel added in.

Jacob sighed. "Commitment to the colonists' cause is not official yet. Let's enjoy the peace we have now. Too bad all disputes can't be settled with a lacrosse game."

Thomas smiled. "Then we hast to teach the colonists and British to play lacrosse, won't we." The men laughed together as they imagined the fun of watching the fictitious game.

"What I don't get is how this all started, why they're so aggrieved with each other. Aren't they from a like tribe?" said Daniel.

"Alas, it befell 'em. It's a done deal now. Blood has already been spilled. There shall no longer be peace between them. May God watch over us and compose that the delegation shall make the right decision for us," said Jacob.

Thomas's eyes grew wide. "Well, Daniel and I best be on our way now, we were told to hasten after service. We hast to finish planting the three sisters today on the farm, corn, beans, and squash. Bid that because they work together to survive and thrive when planted close to each other. I wonder why they're called 3 sisters and not 3 brothers?"

"Probably because sisters have a better sense not to be late, allow us to get going Thomas," said Daniel.

Jacob shook his head.

The crowd of people slowly departed the meeting house and Jacob began his return home. On his way, he passed the large, granite upright Oneida Stone in the center of the village. This sacred "standing stone"—the Oneida were called "People of the Standing Stone"—was also a walking stone, for legend held that it followed the Oneidas whenever they relocated their principal village. He touched the stone lightly. There was a feeling of peace here that transcended his everyday concerns. In the shadow of the stone, Jacob could feel the breath of God and hear the beauty of his creations. He was home. As he walked away from the stone, thoughts of war and upset trundled through his brain like pouring rain, with no intention of stopping.

CHAPTER 5

HOMESICKNESS

Mid February 1777. The chill bit deeper as the sun started to fall below the horizon, looking pinkish. In the darkening, Samuel slouched towards his destination, glum, hands in his coat pocket. His face was drawn and twisted, the face of a man who wanted to weep but could not. The smell announced what Samuel wanted to see before him. He stood with a tear in his eye looking at the body of another friend, Ethan Clark, in a mass grave. With his heart and soul he prayed, Lord, when is this suffering going to end? I know you are with us and Ethan will dwell with you forever, but I pray you to deliver us from these hardships. Amen. Samuel reached down, grabbed a small handful of soft dirt, and let it slowly roll off his hands onto his dear friend. He then headed back to Valley Forge, which he now thought should be named Valley of Death, to etch another notch in his knife handle.

The great killer was not musket balls or freezing temperatures, but illness. Like most wars up till then, typhus, typhoid and dysentery were raging. Much of the sickness came from poor personal hygiene and unhealthy disposal of waste. Disease spread like wildfire in the cramped huts. Washington regularly complained of the failure to eliminate filth in the encampment. The filth included human waste and rotting carcasses of horses. Washington even issued orders concerning the use and care of latrines, but men relieved themselves wherever they wanted. With no wells dug, water was drawn from nearby creeks and nearby Schuylkill River. Men and animals often relieved themselves again and again upstream from where drinking water was taken. Horrible smells finally prompted Washington to take extreme measures. He gave orders that any soldiers who relieved themselves in unapproved areas were to receive five lashes.

A great worry of George Washington's was an outbreak of smallpox. Washington experienced smallpox himself when he was only 19 years old, on an adventure in the West Indies. Smallpox is a dreadful disease that starts with a chill running throughout the body, then within a few days, a rash appears on his skin. In about two days the rash erupts and covers the entire body. Washington wore reminders of the disease on his pockmarked face for the rest of his life; the scars were omitted from his portraits but can be seen on his death mask.

Perhaps the treatment of bleeding a fevered patient left an impression on Washington because he ended the practice. There were other treatments known to decrease inflammation, including medicine, fluids, and a special liquid diet, but Washington knew that prevention with inoculation was the best medicine. Washington was a firm believer in inoculation although it was still relatively new and controversial. This life-saving procedure was first introduced by African slaves. They would harvest puss from the smallpox victim and spread the excretion on fresh cuts to the skin of healthy men. Many soldiers at Valley Forge were vulnerable. The deadly virus became rampant during the worst epidemic of smallpox in American history. About half of the soldiers in the camp were vaccinated. One in five died from the inoculation but the gamble paid off.

Samuel made it back to the camp entrance just as "tap-too" or tattoo was playing on snare drums to signal the end of the workday. A wave of homesickness washed over Samuel as he made his way into camp. He found himself walking toward the Rhode Island Militia to help escape his heavy heart over Ethan's death. Most of the camp was made of continental soldiers but many militias were present, including the 2nd Rhode Island regiment, which was spending winter here. He had not visited the militia until now because he did not want to stir sad memories of his parents who remained in Newport on their family farm. He also was not yet ready to see his younger brother Duncan Fox. It still upset Samuel that Duncan refused to join the continental regulars, choosing instead to enlist in the militia. His brother's main argument for not joining the regulars was similar to that of many colonists, who viewed a standing army as a threat to their rights and a possible future threat to their liberties. Samuel was practical in his thoughts, believing a disciplined, unified standing army was needed to go toe to toe against the British on the battlefield. The militia was great at local defense but they were not disciplined enough to fight off a superpower.

He searched for the Rhode Islanders' brandished flag that proclaimed their commitment to the salvation of liberty as well as a pure white banner, which carried a sheet anchor in the color blue. The sheet anchor is the heaviest anchor on a ship, used only in the foulest of weather to hold the ship fast. The early flag version bore the motto, In te domine speramus, meaning "In God We Hope," but now the blue banner had been adapted to a blue ribbon emblazoned with the word "Hope" above the anchor. The Rhode Island militia was established in 1741 and had sent troops to Queen Anne's War, King George's War, and the French and Indian War before the Revolution. Rhode Island was the smallest colony, barely a speck on the map of British map makers, but their commitment to the Revolution was strong.

Samuel located the Militia huddled around their campfires. Several fifers were playing "Yankee Doodle," a popular tune since the war, although its origins were from the twelfth century. One of the Rhode Islanders immediately noticed Samuel and stood up from his seat on a tree stump near a large fire. "Is that you, Samuel? Joined the regulars I see, the Rhode Island Militia too good for ye?" Samuel barely recognized the man as Abner Smith. The widower Abner, a once robust middle-aged man, had lost more than a few pounds and had a sullen face. Abner ran his hands through his hair and it stuck in clumps, the paths of his fingers still visible right down to the scalp. From under his unkempt brown hair peeked sunken eyes of hazel.

Samuel smirked. "I get to kill more red coats that way."

Abner grinned. "Stay for dinner with us!" Abner coughed and wheezed. "One of the officers bought a few potatoes and salt for the men from the camp followers' market. We mashed it up and mixed it with the fire cake".

Samuel's stomach growled and he did not hesitate. "I never turn down an invite. Besides, it sounds like a feast. It's been a while since I had anything besides plain fire cake." Samuel made himself as comfortable as he could on a large cut log near the fire. Abner tossed a blanket to Samuel to wrap himself with. A small group of militia recognized the Continental uniform and sat down to join the conversation. It became crowded around the fire. More wood was fetched and tossed on the crackling flames, sending sparks into the night air.

Abner grinned. "Ye have such a pretty uniform though I can't ordain it's more comfortable than this." He pointed to his uniform. The militia uniform in contrast to the continental uniform was similar to how Native Americans dressed. They wore a white hunting shirt, ornamented with a great many fringes, somewhat resembling a wagoner's frock. Tied around the waist was a broad belt, to which was attached a tomahawk, the shot bag, and a carved powder horn. Most wore a flapped hat of a reddish hue with a gold cord tied around it.

The logs ablaze settled in the fire pit with a loud crack. A middle-aged, African American dressed as a militiaman approached the fire. The man had a thin face, yet was handsome nonetheless. He had cheekbones high and prominent. Despite his olive skin his nose was all African to match his brown eyes and dark hair. He poured out small spoonfuls of fire cake batter mixed with finely chopped potato on stones close to the fire, just enough batter for one cake per man, then stood looking for an open spot around the crowded campfire to sit. Samuel recognized the man. "Is that you, Cato?"

Cato stared into the eyes of Samuel. Recognition.

"Here is a space." Samuel made room next to himself. As soon as Cato squished in beside him, the words flew out of Samuel. "What news from Newport? I departed before the British ever landed. My parents chose to stay behind to care for the farm. Any word on my younger brother Duncan. He's part of the Rhode Island Militia. Do you know where he is?"

Cato digested the words for a moment. "It is good to see ye, Samuel. I will do my best to answer your questions. I hark the British hast the island on lockdown. Half the population hath left and most of those who keep in Newport fight for the loyalists. That shall change anon. Traffic hath been restrained and the British are taking control of homes, stealing resources, and e'en destroying houses for firewood to survive winter. The British e'en made use of the Redwood Library in town as an officer's club. Should I put me two cents worth, those loyalist traitors are not fit to bear a taper and they are getting what they deserve." Cato drew a long breath. "Thy brother Duncan didst not travel with us and I haven't known a word of him. I hope he is well."

Samuel tossed a small stick into the fire. "I trust my brother is fine. Duncan is stubborn and chooses his own paths, paths that usually turn in the right direction. How do you fare, Cato? I never thought I'd see you dressed as a militiaman."

Cato's eyes lit up. "Never thought I'd see the day myself, but war is upon us. I serve of my own accord. I do compose them to pay for the burning of Falmouth. The bastards' navy bombarded Falmouth from morning till evening. After the bombardment ended, they dispatched a landing party into town and set fire to the buildings that hadn't been destroyed. To attack innocent civilians so. It just ain't right."

Samuel held his hands out to the warmth of the fire. He frowned into the flames. "We will make them pay for every vile act they commit. I'm glad to see ye here in the cause for liberty, Cato. May the Lord bless and protect you."

Cato exhaled slowly, "Thank you, Samuel, may the Lord bless and protect ye as well." The fire cakes were grabbed from the hot stone when they finished cooking. Samuel passed his hot cake from hand to hand till it cooled enough to eat. He answered a few questions about serving as a Continental soldier to the gathering around the fire. Satisfied that serving as a Continental soldier was not that remarkable, they quickly shifted the conversation to the homes they missed and what they would be doing now if they were back there.

Cato Bannister was a slave from the descendants of a wealthy merchant and slave trader, John Bannister II from Newport, Rhode Island. He left an apprenticeship to Mr. Elkana Humphrey of Barrington, Rhode Island, who would receive interest paid to him for his slave's use. Cato was appraised at a little over 100 pounds. Cato joined the 1st Rhode Island Regiment as an early enlistee. Among the Rhode Island militia, a good number of African American's were in the mix. In the war councils George Washington held during the early spring and summer of 1775, it was decided to "Reject negroes altogether" for the Continental army. Despite Washington's prejudice, the need for manpower to help fill the depleted ranks of the Continental Army was great. He started admitting African Americans with "prior military experience" in January 1776. He also extended enlistment terms to all free African Americans the following year. At Valley Forge, it is estimated that 700 African American soldiers were encamped, along with an unknown number that filled support roles. They came mostly from the Northern States of Massachusetts, Connecticut, and Rhode Island. The 1st Rhode Island Regiment recently merged into the 2nd Rhode Island Regiment and Rhode Island Militia officers were returning to Rhode Island to raise a new 1st Rhode Island Regiment, a battalion consisting entirely of freed slaves.

Around the crackle of the fire, the men yearned for home. "I'd be sitting near the fireplace at home, with my dog at my feet, eating a delicious apple, about to nod off," said Samuel.

"I'd be putting the children to bed about now, probably after telling them a story from my intrepid youth," said Abner. "Then to bed myself, happily dreaming of a pretty lass. It's alright lads, I'm a widow you see."

"I'd be having free time about now after my master's shoes had been polished," Cato said. He stood up, brushed dirt off his rear. "Using the time for practicing my math lessons, making sure to hast time to read my Bible. Had we chosen to stay, I wonder if we be dreaming about life in the army right now? I wonder."

Abner looked up at Cato. "I won't aye forget this winter, I shall say to thee."

Cato smiled as he moved a large bundle of sticks closer to the fire. "I shall bet ye shall miss my cooking when I'm gone."

Abner grinned. "Thy cooking is not half bad, Cato." He winked. "Just would we had some beer to swallow it down with tonight." Abner raised his mug of ice-cold water. "No beer of any sort in days." Samuel grabbed a stick from the bundle of wood Cato brought over and tossed it into the flames. He watched the stick catch fire to join the flames.

A sudden wintry cold gust of wind howled through the camp, and a freezing rain began to spit. Samuel came as close to the fire as he could, nearly burning the blanket. He could feel his lungs fill with a sharp cold each time he breathed in. The bleak grey clouds above now reflected Samuel's mood perfectly. He finished his fire cake slowly, relishing every bite. He could not help but think what mother probably served at her table tonight. He dusted the crumbs off his blanket. Time to get back to my cabin and what little warmth it is. "Well, boys, time to go." He paused to yawn copiously behind his hand. "You take care of yourselves and on the next proper occasion due be careful of a bayonet charge." He said this in good humor, knowing what most continental regulars thought about the militia. Handing the blanket back to Abner, he bid farewell to his fellow Rhode Islanders. He knew it may be true that Rhode Islanders are the first to complain about their state, but they're just as quick to demand respect for it. Rhode Island may be the smallest colony, only a speck on a map, but they were proud of where they came from and proud of their fight for the cause of liberty.

CHAPTER 6
THE SHADOW OF DEATH

The grey clouds seemed to have moved in to stay. Not a speck of sun had been seen for weeks. Another day of snow shifted to icy cold rain. Samuel stared up at the roof of the cabin listening to the steady pattern of freezing rain upon his hut, droplets scattering what little sleep he received. He listened till the drops stopped. The cabin with its stove gave decent enough warmth from the frigid weather. Samuel was not cold but he wished for a thick bed rug over his worn blanket. He slowly removed his blanket and dressed himself. He splashed cold water on his face, which did nothing to take the fog from his head due to lack of sleep. Tea! If he could not have breakfast this morning at least a strong tea would do. An icy breeze struck him as soon as he closed the door to the cabin. He went over to the closest campfire pit and tossed a few hunks of wood into orange embers, igniting the flames. He filled a copper tea kettle with water and placed it on a rock just outside the flames. Slowly his cabin mates began to emerge to join him around the fire. Many rested their heads on the palm of their hands, gazes downward. Spirits were low among the men, shivering, hungry and not to mention bored.

Boredom was occasionally relieved by work assignments in the encampment. There was no end of labor that needed to be done. Although it was winter, odds and ends still needed to be tasked in camp, the wood had to be cut, fires continuously fed, and foraging for food that never ended. The most unliked job was to transport the sick to the hospital. It was physically as well as emotionally draining. Samuel's work detail would begin soon. Unfortunately for him, his name came for labor today at the camp's most dreaded assignment.

The water was piping hot in the kettle after Samuel took it off the hot coals just before boiling. He placed a tiny cloth sack filled with tea leaves in it and let it sit for a few minutes, then poured a cup for himself and sipped it greedily. After the first cup, he poured another. The tea did help remove some of the fog from his head. He gave the rest of the tea kettle away after his two full cups to the men joining him around the fire. Rising from his log seat, he said a quick goodbye to his cabin mates. There were now two fewer than had previously arrived at the camp, both recent notches on his knife handle. One died from high fever two weeks ago, practically overnight, the other suffered in delusional fever at the hospital till the grim reaper came for him.

Samuel moved out on the heavily rutted dirt paths toward his assignment. His shoes crunched thin ice sheets formed over the grooves made in the dirt from wagon wheels. At least finding shoes was no longer a supply problem; the dead fed an endless supply now. He moved gingerly, mindful of preventing a twisted ankle. It did not take long to reach the ramshackle duty station—A simple tent with a clerk that would sign out the equipment his detail would need.

"Ehem!" a voice called out.

Samuel turned to see George Washington. Washington had the look and figure of a man beset with grief.

"Good morrow to thee. I hope thou hast not forgotten the conversation about reporting accurate details about the men in camp," said Washington.

"I have not forgotten, General. It certainly has not been a leisurely walk. Although we are cold, fatigued, hungry, and want clothes, we are still resolved to see this through. Although many deem tis only through Holy Providence that we endure." Samuel felt the weight of his lead cross around his neck briefly. "If I may be so bold, I fear the situation is getting worse. The men gripe over their pay being inconsistent. Many are broke and simply want money to send home, as they have been unable to continue their trade because of service to the army. Many poor men enlisted and negotiated in good faith and joined as free men. They see the army as not fulfilling their part of the bargain."

Washington frowned. "I do blame Congress for the issue about the pay for the men. I have beseeched Congress in earnest to uphold their promises. I am most unhappy with the situation yet can doth very little. I see desertion is definitely growing. I'm trying to strike a delicate balance 'twixt harshness and leniency. I hast reduced the number of lashes required to discipline a misdeed, yet I shall not tolerate dissension or mutiny. Ringleaders shall be executed to set an example. Duty and honor must prevail." Samuel nodded and Washington continued, "Officers are complaining to me that the men are at their wit's end. That they are cursed and cussed at. They are not being shown the respect for place. What doth thou say about this?"

"The mood in camp is that officers don't feel the common soldiers' hardships at present. They try to be gentlemen. They try to mimic European ways yet they're Americans. Perhaps if officers toiled more side by side with the men. They may earn their proper respect."

"Well, if that be so, as of now officers will travail more, and would they be unjust they may start receiving the lashes. Officers need to be the bedrock of this army. The men must discover respect yet respect must also be earned. Tell me, what doth thou receive is the most pressing import in camp."

"The men are bored."

Washington did not act surprised. "I agree. Horseplay is running amuck. I hear the constant random firing of muskets! Seldom a day passes without someone accidentally shot by a friend. I will see to more entertainment for the men. Perhaps a few wicket bats can be made up in due haste. Officers and their ladies have approached me recently to put on a production of Cato at the Bake House. A favorite story of mine. It recounts Cato's noble yet vain efforts to save the remnants of the Roman Republic from the usurping arms of the tyrant Caesar. When vice prevails, impious men must bear sway. It may most well entertain and inspire the men."

"The men are hungry," Samuel said. "They'd eat the cabin wood if they could."

"As for the food shortages, the surrounding farms hast had a bountiful harvest yet they would rather smuggle their food to the British than bargain with what we hast to offer 'em. We hast to be tough on 'em yet tread carefully. I have beseeched Congress for aid, yet little has been coming. Be at peace. I am working on this issue."

Washington shook Samuel's hand. "Thy insight is valuable to me. Alas, I'm in haste. I shall continue to bid upon you. I pray you remain safe in body and firm-set to the cause of liberty."

"Yes, General."

Samuel watched as Washington departed. Washington walked slowly, shoulders back, eyes frequently looking over the camp. It gave Samuel comfort to know how much Washington was concerned about his men. He respected the sacrifices of Washington's endless work. Washington could have retired and read about the Revolution in the paper, instead, he fought tirelessly in the cause of Liberty. A cause that was struggling at Valley Forge.

Samuel arrived just outside the duty tent to see a continental soldier leaning against a boulder with arms folded, kicking at clumps of dead grass.

"Yee must be Samuel. Privilege to meet ya. My name is Joseph Plumb Martin. I'll be joining the labor with you today. I'm from the Continental 17th Regiment also known as the 8th Connecticut Regiment." He shook Samuel's hand, then let go a hacking cough.

"I am Samuel. It is good to meet you. Quite a cough. You ain't too ill for this are you?"

"Well, fit as a fiddle they would say, although a mite worn out. It still gets the job done."

Joseph appeared a bit pale and rundown. Joseph once could have been called handsome but he now looked haggard and thin. His brown hair was unkempt under a thick wool cap and his brown eyes a deep pool of misery.

Samuel and Joseph were handed a well-worn makeshift litter to carry the sick men to the hospital. The litter had long carrying poles that hung with ropes, a wooden hammock. A wagon, with a driver, was to take them to their stops. Their assigned duty was to use the litter to transport the frail, unfortunate individuals into and out of the wagon. The wagon acting as an ambulance would then deliver the sick to one of the hospitals, then go back to the camp to collect more.

As they waited for the wagon to assist them, Samuel told Joseph about his life in Newport and Joseph talked a little about his life in Milford, Connecticut. Samuel learned that Joseph was well educated, his father had studied at Yale and Joseph was able to receive a well-rounded education, that of a gentleman. Joseph was living with his grandparents when war broke out. He wanted to enlist earlier in the war but his grandparents refused. Finally, he vowed to run away and join the navy as a privateer unless they allowed him to join. They finally relented and at 15 Joseph signed up with the Connecticut militia in June 1776. Joseph shared a similar rebellious spirit with Samuel and they took to liking each other right away.

The wagon driver, a civilian that went by the name of Ebenezer, wore a weathered farmer's face and a perpetual scowl. The driver held a list with camp locations for pick-up of the sickly. The beat-up wagon was small and was moved by a chestnut-colored mare. The animal was no stallion; it looked moth-eaten and old. Connected to the earth by hoof, they would still be indebted to the horse for making the burden easier. The wagon kicked out clumps of frozen mud as it rumbled off to work.

Together, Samuel and Joseph approached the first transport of the day, to collect a Thomas Montgomery, a Continental regular who had definitely seen better days. Thomas's friends parted a path in the cabin to let the litter through. Thomas, a narrow-faced, young fellow appeared pale and ghost-like. The gaze he turned upon the litter carriers was so despairing that Samuel nearly gasped. Thomas was struggling to breathe and barely holding on for life. Samuel and Joseph quickly put Thomas on the litter. They gently carried him to the wagon and covered Thomas in a pile of blankets. Immediately the wagon departed with Samuel remaining in the back of the wagon to steady Thomas on the ride while Joseph sat beside the driver. The driver tried to move as gently as possible, but the road made the wagon jostled back and forth towards the hospital. Thomas moaned softly.

They were headed to America's first true military hospital, constructed for that purpose and built at Yellow Springs, originally a popular health spa about 10 miles west of the encampment. Approximately 300 sick men were held in the large three-story wood building. Dr. Bodo Otto, an elderly German, and his two physician sons ran the hospital under the direction of Dr. Samuel Kennedy who was appointed senior surgeon of military hospitals. Many temporary hospitals were built in the region of Eastern Pennsylvania, using at least 50 barns, dwellings, churches, or meetinghouses. These makeshift hospitals were mostly undermanned, desperately in need of medical supplies, and gross breeding grounds for disease.

After arrival, Samuel and Joseph carried Thomas towards the front entrance. A weary-faced woman met them to help take charge of Thomas. She had her hair high in a knot, parted in the center, and waved back on both sides of her brow. She was plainly dressed in a red gown and a blue petticoat was worn over a second hooped petticoat which kept her skirt out.

Joseph's eyes bulged wide, "Mary, is that you?" He coughed. Joseph turned to Samuel speaking fast. "A brave one is her. She's known for carrying water to the thirsty soldiers even with bullets flying. Her husband in part of the artillery, and who was then attached to a cannon in a battle. I witnessed her helping attend with her husband at the cannon. While in the act of reaching for a cartridge and having one of her feet as far ere the other as she could step, a cannon shot from the foe passed directly 'twixt her legs without doing any other damage than carrying away all the lower part of her petticoat. She didn't e'en flinch, just continued to help fire the cannon. Some call her Molly Pitcher."

The daughter of a New Jersey dairy farmer, Mary Ludwig Hays McCauley was born in 1754. She was employed as a domestic servant to a middle-class household and married a barber named William. When the Revolutionary War began, her husband William enlisted in the Pennsylvania Artillery as a gunner. Becoming a camp follower, Mary joined her husband on the campaign. The Continental Army followed precedents set by ancient and contemporary military forces in developing its own military community. There have been camp followers as long as there have been armies and they took risks similar to what a soldier endures.

"Gentlemen!" Mary snapped, interrupting Joseph. She did not seem in the mood for any conversation but she did give a hint of a smile when Joseph spoke the name, Molly Pitcher. She stood there tired-eyed. There's a certain amount of tiredness that equates to madness; she looked close to it. She drew a deep breath and softened her tone. "Gentlemen, if you would follow me, please." They followed her through the cramped and crowded hospital. The sound of hacking and coughing of poor souls could be heard everywhere. Samuel and Joseph gently removed Thomas from the litter and placed him on an available wooden cart. Molly made him comfortable by simply placing a blanket over him. Molly looked up at the men with a plaintive face. "We are in desperate need of medicine and supplies. We are short since nearly all we use was previously imported from the British. If you have any hidden stash we desperately need, maybe some mercury compound, lavender spirits, sage, or cream of tartar?" Samuel and Joseph both shook their heads and lowered them. They had nothing to give but their service today.

A doctor soon looked over at Thomas. He carried a leather doctor's bag. Doctors at this period of time had more in common with medieval barbers than today's doctors. Many believed that illness was caused by an imbalance of the humors, which were blood, yellow bile, black bile, and phlegm. Because of this belief, you either drained fluids away or added them. Contained in his doctor's bag were implements that today would be considered cruel. Tools designed to bleed, sweat, and purge infected fluids from the body. The doctor without delay tried to get Thomas to ingest an ugly-looking concoction made from a slurry mix of molasses, vinegar, and butter. He was unsuccessful in getting the patient to swallow even a drop. Shaking his head after looking at Thoma's shoulder, the doctor looked up at Mary with a blanketed stare, signaling to her there was nothing he could do. Mary fought hard to hold back tears. Samuel and Joseph had seen enough; they quickly gathered the litter and departed to the waiting wagon to begin collecting more sick.

It will never be known just how many unfortunate lives became seriously ill during the Valley Forge encampment and how many died of these illnesses. An estimated total of 3,000 souls died at camp or in quick-and-dirty hospitals. This count held the highest death rate of any Continental Army encampment, and even higher than most military engagements of the war.

It was rumored that in the darkest hours of valley forge that George Washington, Father of the American Nation, was found in a solitary place praying to the ultimate Father, the almighty God.

In vocal prayer, he beseeched the Lord to interpose with divine aid to save the American States. On his knees alone, with his sword on one side and his hat lying beside him, his hands clasped and raised to heaven. Whether this event was real or imagined, it symbolized a people who knew that it was not enough to depend on their own courage and righteousness, that they must also seek help from God. The revolution could have ended with Valley Forge. Instead of an ending, prayers were about to be answered.

CHAPTER 7

ANSWERED PRAYERS

Samuel rose after a fitful slumber to the feeling of cold air. The fire must be low again. There were fewer men to staff the fire. Nearly half the original occupants now were either dead, dying, or at hospitals. The dead would be more notches cut into his knife handle. He let out a long yawn in the pale morning light, got up, and placed more wood into the fire. Only an hour ago the blackness was absolute, but now the morning mist was visible. Waking up was no longer the pleasure once remembered. If he could, Samuel would remain in bed hibernating like a bear waiting until spring. Morning reveille sounded with a shrill call from bugles followed immediately with drums roaring for a call to arms. The men stumbled to get dressed and out the door as quickly as possible with muskets in tow. Officers appeared and hollered for the men to move quickly to an assembly area just outside the camp. A roll of thunder. The clouds dropped a light cold rain just as they finished forming into a jangled formation.

George Washington stood fading the Army. He ignored the rain although it dripped on his face. His breath was visible in the frigid air.

The men hunched against the cold faces haggard but excited to hear what he had to say. "I have the pleasure of introducing to you Baron Friedrich Wilhelm Ludolf Gerhard Augustin von Steuben, who has traveled far to volunteer his services. He served in the Prussian army with distinction as an aide-de-camp to Frederick the Great. May I also introduce Louis de Pontiere, his aide de camp, and Pierre Ettienne Duponceau, his military secretary, I have appointed Baron von Steuben temporary Inspector General." Steuben stepped out to salute Washington, then moved to address the crowd. Steuben was a heavyset man and striking in the martial aspect. Steuben appeared to be a personification of Mars, the ancient Roman God of War. His uniform was perfectly cut with a giant eight-pointed silver star on his chest, etched with the word fidelitous and he wore extravagant ornate holsters for his pistols. He took off his hat to address the crowd. The rain pasted his hair to his scalp.

"Désolé je ne parle pas anglais. Je parle Prussian et français. Je parle français maintenant pour mieux traduire. . . ." A young-faced Colonel Alexander Hamilton translated after Baron Steuben finished speaking: "Sorry I do not speak English. I speak both Prussian and French. I speak French now to better translate. I wish to thank Washington for the honor that has been given to me. I will be traveling around the camp inspecting and talking with you shortly. I look forward to fighting with you in the cause of Liberty. As your Benjamin Franklin, at the signing of the Declaration of Independence, notably said, you must all hang together, or assuredly you shall all hang separately if this rebellion fails. We are in it to the end, so give us liberty or give us death!" After the translation, Steuben raised his fist in the air and shouted, "Huzzah!"

The crowd of soldiers responded back with shouts of "Huzzah!" repeated several times in a vibrant roar. Afterward, the men were dismissed. While brave, the American Army was in desperate need of discipline and training. There were no regular roll calls. Orders prohibiting gambling, fighting, selling Army equipment, and wandering away from the camp were routinely ignored. The new Army didn't know how to march in ranks or maneuver on the battlefield. The bayonet, a crucial weapon for battlefield success, was used mostly to cook over a fire.

Steuben listened during the interviews he conducted with soldiers and absorbed the situation like a thirsty sponge soaking up water. What he found was an army short of everything, except spirit. The spirit made up for the poor military standards. He was quoted as saying "No European army could have held together in such circumstances." Now, if he could get the military standards to meet their spirits the army would be unstoppable. He knew the army would not train like soldiers he was used to training. The American soldier was fiercely independent in his nature and thought differently than their European ancestors. In another quote Baron Steuben remarked, "You say to your soldier, 'Do this' and he does it. But I am obliged to say to the American, 'This is why you ought to do this' and then he does it.'"

Baron Steuben had a few challenges ahead besides the need to rely on French translators from Washington's aides-de-camp John Laurens and Alexander Hamilton. At this time, each colony used divergent training methods by various European countries. The army was far from uniform, but at least most knew how to fire a weapon. As newly appointed Inspector General, Steuben's task was to create one standard method, thus coordinating the entire Continental Army. Steuben fastidiously set to work. Steuben assembled a select unit of men consisting of Continentals, including George Washington's personal guard unit and militiamen from each state, about 120 men total, to personally teach them and afterward they would demonstrate each new lesson to their respective units. He would create mirrors of himself minus his flamboyant and cussing nature to quicken the training time.

Samuel was chosen by his regiment as one of the volunteers to be personally instructed by Steuben. He couldn't help but think

Washington played a part in his selection. Samuel stood in a dead, yellow grass clearing with the large group of chosen men. A larger group of officers and sergeants stood a little away surrounding the model company to observe and learn. Samuel shivered in the cold and rubbed his hands waiting for Steuben to arrive. He did arrive dressed as sharply and flamboyantly as ever, wearing a large medal of his own design. Steuben first called the men to attention. They barely had a clue of the true position of attention, but he ignored it for now. He then inspected the half-naked men's uniforms. He removed and tossed to the ground anything that did not belong in regulations. In broken English, he cussed a bit, mostly in humor, or at least the men took it that way. After the uniform inspection, he demonstrated movements without firearms. "Firm and precise movements, men!" was translated. They were taught to keep shoulders square to the front and kept back, and the hands hanging down the sides, with the palms close to the thighs. "To the Right- Face! To the Left- Face! Attention! Rest!" The men stumbled through the exercises for hours until they reached a basic understanding. They would likely march in their sleep that night.

The next day Steuben added firearms to the drills. The translators shouted instructions in English. "Shoulder-Firelock!, Present-Arms!, Charge-Bayonet! Samuel sweated through the positions trying not to knock out anyone beside him or accidentally pierce someone with his bayonet in the compact formation. Each motion was delivered with one perfect beat between each motion. Next, the men were handed wooden drill flints and blank cartridges to simulate firing. "Poise-Firelock! Two motions, Cock-Firelock! Two motions, Take Aim! One motion, Fire! One motion." They drilled tirelessly to be able to load and fire 3-4 shots per minute in a tight formation.

Late evening came. The select unit was finally released, fed, and sent to bed. In exhausted, deep sleep the men did not stir. Steuben wasn't lucky enough to go to bed; instead, he continued to work late into the night, writing page-by-page, staying only several days ahead of the whole army. He worked tirelessly to create drill plans that could be understood simply. A straightforward plan would create uniform maneuvers and discipline more rapidly. His drill plans were simplified so the men he was teaching would learn in the quickest possible time. In this way, reliable maneuvers and discipline were given to the army rapidly. Day by day he was slowly shaping and molded the Continental ragtag army into a professional army.

Finally, the select unit training was completed with the addition of bayonet drills. No longer were the bayonets to be used for cooking but for killing. Samuel pushed through the weariness that crept into his arms and legs. He was striking at a straw dummy representing the British. With overzealousness, he pierced through the dummy and his entire musket slipped from his fingers going through the dummy as well, landing on the ground. "Oh hell!," Steuben exclaimed in broken English with his eyes popping open. Samuel turned to look directly at the vivacious Steuben, his face turned red with embarrassment. His heart pounded as he glanced at the dummy. "Garder une prise ferme lorsque vous poignardez," Steuben spoke in French with a smile. "Keep a tight grip when you stab," Colonel Hamilton translated. Steuben picked up the musket and demonstrated the strike then handed it back to Samuel. Steuben and Hamilton abruptly moved on and Samuel continued the stabbing drill, this time with a tighter grip. Steuben's training was challenging and exhausting but Samuel was proud of his new discipline and his confidence was boosted. He was able to report the training progress of the select unit personally to Washington.

In a few weeks, the model men knew what they were doing, Steuben released them to teach others along with the officers and sergeants that observed. Soon there was the drilling of large masses including entire regiments and brigades. Officers were instructed to keep it simple, to be mild on the men, and punish only those with willful neglect. Up to this point, the American officers, following the British example, did not work directly in training the men. They thought it ungentlemanlike and beneath them. Steuben showed them a new model by working directly with the common soldier. Washington highly preferred this model especially because it closely corresponded with Samuel's thoughts about officers and the enlisted. These officers initially felt threatened by this practice, as well as by the seemingly unlimited powers of Steuben's office but the men loved him for working with them directly as well as his use of profanity (in several different languages), making him popular among the soldiers. The American officers began following Steuben's example and it helped grow unit cohesion. The officers and men worked long hours in the harsh winter weather, transforming themselves. This army, once a rabble, a flock of scared sheep, was becoming a professional army ready to go toe to toe with the British superpower. They were now lions ready for the hunt. A dangerous prey they sought indeed. Lions fighting was a brutal scene with only one victor emerging.

George Washington was pleased with the positive results for the army and Steuben was removed from his temporary position and officially promoted to the Inspector General. The Baron was a puzzle. The man himself was pompous and his uniforms were like state props but he succeeded. If Washington is the Father of our country I believe Steuben is the Father of the American Military.

CHAPTER 8

CONFABULATION WITH HAMILTON

Samuel sat on a damp, wooden stump cleaning his musket. He went over the words from Baron von Steuben's instructions in his head about the importance of musket maintenance. Muskets were notorious for the amount of maintenance they needed, all maladies made worse by actually firing these weapons. Samuel took a boiling teapot off hot coals. The pot was not for tea, but to pour down the barrel of his weapon. After he poured the hot water down the barrel carefully, he took his oily rag and capped the end of the barrel. He shook vigorously trying not to burn himself. After a few shakes, he poured out the blackest water imaginable. He repeated the process, with just enough water to make the barrel finally run clear. He wiped the weapon down with his oily rag then started working on the rust spots with a mix of cold campfire ash and spit. After he finished his musket, he moved to his flintlock pistol.

With both weapons cleaned he stood up to admire his work. They will definitely pass any surprise inspection, he thought to himself. Best mine looks good when I'm the one giving the surprise inspection tomorrow. Just then a gentle hand tapped his shoulder from behind. Samuel turned around and looked directly at Colonel Alexander Hamilton, interpreter for Baron von Steuben and aide to George Washington. The young Hamilton was fair-skinned with reddish-brown hair, his eyes were a deep-set blue, almost violet. He had a long Roman-type nose, with a strong jaw and firm mouth. Hamilton's uniform was crisp and perfectly clean. Samuel stood up to attention and saluted. Hamilton smiled, "At ease. You have done well, Samuel. The Baron wanted me to tell you he is proud of thy soldiery, especially your ability to teach thy skills once you have learned them. With the Baron's blessing and your regiment's, you are hereby promoted to sergeant." Hamilton handed Samuel a small patch of red cloth that would later need to be sewn on the right shoulder of Samuel signifying his rank. Samuel took a deep breath, absorbing for a moment his achievement. Samuel stuttered, "Th-Th-Thank you, sir, I am honored."

Hamilton shook his hand then took a seat on a log near the orange coals that Samuel had been using to heat water and motioned Samuel to sit down. Samuel returned to his wooden stump close by. "I envy you, Samuel. Soon you will see future action with the army. I fear that as an aide to Washington and because my mother taught me French that I may not be able to leave my job as a translator for the Baron. I'm yearning to be on the front lines fighting for liberty." Samuel once thought battle exciting, but he knew now the exciting part was what you remembered when you looked back after the battle was fought. Not sure what to say, Samuel politely nodded. He knew little about Hamilton but he did hear the rumor that Hamilton was a bastard child born out of wedlock from the West Indies, but Samuel could care less. It was a man's heart and experience that was the most important trait for men to follow. Hamilton continued, "Tell me about thy family, Samuel." Samuel revealed to Hamilton a brief description of his family and about his love for his mother's cooking. Hamilton reached down, grabbed a stick, and poked the orange coals. "Did your family support thy enlistment?" Samuel mentioned his family's support and how his brother Duncan had joined the militia, refusing to join the Continentals because of his beliefs about a powerful central government leading to trouble. Hamilton considered his thoughts. "Surely, I believe we need a strong independent Continental Army or surely we will lose this war. Your brother may not serve with the Continentals but he does serve. The militia serves an important role, more so if their muskets would take better aim."

Hamilton removed his tricorn hat, placing it on the log next to him. Passion flared in his eyes. "I have been thinking hard about the political situation. Congress is too preoccupied with its own interests to function properly. How can we hope for success in our European negotiations, particularly with France, if the nations of Europe have no confidence in the wisdom and vigor of our Continental Government? If Congress is powerless to raise and appropriate money to supply its own army, what good are they?"

Samuel rubbed the top of his head, combing his dirty fingers through his hair, "I see what you mean. We suffer needlessly while General Howe and the Brits are living large in Philadelphia because Congress can't move fast enough to help. They need to stop arguing political intrigue and support the defenders of liberty that are in the field."

Hamilton nodded in agreement. "We have beseeched Congress with all due haste but the politicians do not understand the needs of an army. I do believe they will learn quickly which is sensitive to our needs." Hamilton returned his hat to his head and rose. "I could talk politics all day, but unfortunately I have more tasks at hand. Our adjournment comes not a moment too soon. Thank you for your service with the Continental Army. I'll be putting in a good word for you with Major Caleb Gibbs, head of Washington's Guard, or the LifeGuard as the men prefer to call it. It seems they are a few short in their ranks." Samuel's mouth twitched, fighting back a smile. It felt like forever since he last smiled. Finally, the battle was lost and his lips stretched into one.

Hamilton enjoyed looking at the grin on Samuel's face, and could not prevent his own from joining. "Well, to liberty, however, it is provided, though I think it up to the strength of our army." Hamilton reached out and shook Samuel's hand.

"I have witnessed much suffering and thanks to the Almighty I am still here. I may be a plain country boy but I ain't no fool. I know in the end that it is the love of God that I pray reverently to aid the cause of liberty and the determination of men's spirit that shall bring us to victory." Hamilton stood for a moment, clearly impressed with Samuel's words.

Hamilton grinned. "Maybe they were wrong in your promotion to sergeant; it should have been as an officer. I shall compose my leave now yet I would enjoy more conversation in the future if time allows as I know my friend Washington would as well." Hamilton departed.

Samuel sat for a while pondering his conversation with Hamilton, then returned to his cabin. Samuel was impressed with Hamilton. He believed Hamilton was a deep thinker that spoke passionately about politics. Definitely a good man to share a pint with. As Samuel considered his thoughts the wind began to blow strongly. He began hearing thunder, great hollow booms that seemed to roll in from nowhere. The drumming of hail began clicking on the frozen ground. Samuel made his escape quickly to his cabin.

After putting his weapons away Samuel pulled out a small sewing kit from his belongings and wasted no time sewing on the red cloth to the right shoulder of his uniform, identifying himself as a sergeant. Sergeants were the backbone of the army. In battle, these noncommissioned officers were responsible for closing the gaps in the battle lines caused by casualties as well as encouraging men to fire rapidly with aimed volley fire. Samuel considered himself up for the task of sergeant and looked forward to his new role.

The cabin was empty with the exception of William Anthony, whose friends called him Bill, and who sat on the floor sharpening his bayonet near the fire. William did not even lookup. He was a new replacement for his regiment. He was a thin man with dirty, blonde hair and deep blue eyes. Bill was undersized, about a foot shorter than average. Samuel figured Bill must have gone through a lot, for Bill always wore a scowl. At times, Samuel tried to ponder Bill's mind to figure out what troubled Bill. He failed miserably and always received a sharp rebuke when getting too deep about it in conversation. There was no way to puzzle out such an unyielding man or so he thought. Bill continued to sharpen away with his sharpening stone. All the men missing or dead had been replaced in the cabin, but one. Recruitment in the winter had been poor. The states were dilatory in filling their battalions. The cabin mates may not have all been there from the beginning but they shared a common bond of soldiery, made even stronger by the rigorous training drills of Baron Steuben. When musket balls start flying, egos are stripped away, and it becomes about your brother to your left and your brother to your right. Together to stand and fight. It's a bond unlike any other.

As the men from the cabin returned from their various duties and drills, there was no mistaking the red patch on Samuel's uniform. Samuel received a plethora of back slaps and many words of congratulations, along with comments such as, "It's about time they see fit to promote you" and "I would have bet my pay if I had any." There would be no cheap, diluted alcohol for the men to celebrate with tonight. They would do better than that. Spiced rum was fetched from some hidden supply to honor the promotion. A bottle was opened and the men passed it about toasting Samuel, then another bottle, then another. The men laughed and sang, forgetting for the moment their troubles. Even Bill's scowl came off for a short moment. A pocket fiddle was produced then music and singing began. Some men hilariously attempted to dance in the cramped quarters. Sweat streaked the dirt off their faces with their exertion. They sang in drunken harmony.

The land where freedom reigns shall still
Be masters of the main,
In giving laws and freedom
To subject France and Spain;
And all the isles o'er ocean spread
Shall tremble and obey,
The prince who rules by Freedom's laws
In North America.

God bless this maiden climate,
And through her vast domain
May hosts of heroes cluster
That scorn to wear a chain.
And blast the venal sycophants
Who dare our rights betray;
Assert yourselves, yourselves, yourselves
For brave America,

Lift up your hearts, my heroes,
And swear with proud disdain,
The wretch that would ensnare you
Shall spread his net in vain;
Should Europe empty all her force,
We'd meet them in array,
And shout huzza, huzza, huzza
For brave America.

(A variation of "Free America" These words are by Dr. Joseph Warren, one of the original Minutemen. Warren sent Paul Revere to Lexington to warn John Adams and John Hancock of the British advance, setting Revere on his famous ride.)

Already exhausted from the Baron's training and plenty of late-night debaucheries, the men began to wane. Samuel yawned first, followed around the room with mouths gaped open one after another. The pink-eyed and slouching men knew they may not be the straightest men in formation or drills tomorrow, but it was worth it for the escape provided. They dozed off one by one.

CHAPTER 9
AS BUSY AS A BEE

Despite the morning light coming through a window, the room was still dark. Several candles fought back the shadows, giving just enough light to read by. Washington was at his desk, quill pen in hand, writing another letter to Congress. He was frustrated and he dipped the pen aggressively. His army was still not getting what was promised. He was committed to the cause of liberty, but he felt the spirit of the Revolution from Congress was losing its backbone. He thought to himself with a short sigh, Congress forgets we shall all be hung for treason if the revolution fails. Supplies and men are not a crave, yet essential to win this war. Blast these politicians. If only I could I would drag them by the ears and have 'em visit hither and see the plight of the army, then they would be more inclined to acquiesce. He finished the letter then sealed it with wax and handed it off to an aide to have the letter sent immediately. He sat back down at his desk to continue writing correspondence. It was a comfortable, well-made chair. He originally wanted to live in a log cabin, like his men at camp, but it soon became apparent it would not work as a headquarters for the army. It was too small for administration so he chose a modest borrowed house outside of camp.

Besides helping the army survive Valley Forge, there was no shortage of individuals eager to depose Washington's position as commander of the army. Opponents in Congress and some in the army spoke behind his back, disobeyed orders, and tried to undermine Washington's leadership. Washington was glad for his unwavering and loyal friends that helped him face down the recent Conway Cabal, a never-hatched plot aimed at forcing Washington to give up command of the Continental Army to Horatio Lloyd Gates.

At fifty, Gates was five years older than Washington and had technically more military experience. His leadership skills were lacking. He selfishly and eagerly took credit for the American victory in the Battle of Saratoga, even though he arrived at the end to claim the lion's share of the victory, while Gen. Philip Schuyler had done most of the planning, and Benedict Arnold and Daniel Morgan had done all the fighting, facts barely discernible in Gates's dispatches.

A gentle knock at the door. "Come in," Washington spoke absently. His wife, Martha, and forever sweetheart, walked in. She was 5 feet tall, slightly plump, with light brown eyes that appeared hazel to some. Her brown hair now was frosted with grey. In Washington's eyes, his wife would always remain stunning, but it was her wit and wisdom he fell in love with.

She looked down into his eyes. "George," she spoke softly, "if you do not have letters yet that are needed for copying, I'd like to visit the men at the hospitals today. I know you are busy, my dear, but I would like to see you take a break from your desk and accompany me if convenient."

Washington laid his pen down. "You go, my dear, I will be engaged all day." He reached over and touched her hands lightly with his. "Would I hast not made it clear, Martha, I appreciate all that you hast done to help me and I'm sure the soldiers appreciate your kindness to 'em, especially the socks you knit for 'em." She blushed then bent over and kissed him on the forehead.

"Then I shall be on my way." Martha quietly departed and Washington remained hard at work. Besides correspondence to write, there were military orders to compose, plenty of dispatches to read.

The sun never came out fully. The sky was cast in dismal grey, but Washington was able to blow out most of the candles in the room. At about noon, the door knocked. Steuben walked in with Hamilton. Steuben was not as flamboyant today, well at least no medal hung from his neck. He wore a grey frock coat, a cream-colored vest with matching breeches, with white lace ornamental frill on the front of his shirt and cuffs. Washington continued to sit in his chair as the men approached. Steuben spoke in French, "Le général Washington, vous remercie encore de......"

Hamilton translated: "General Washington, thank you again for the opportunity to serve the cause of liberty. Regardless of what the men hast gone through they continue to hast spirit. I report that training is going better than expected, the model company is now dispersed to train. Camp hygiene is not up to standards yet, but at least I do not step in shite on my inspections."

Washington nodded. "Grammercy for thy report, Baron, as always it is short and to the point. Say to me shall the men be prepared by spring?"

In broken English Steuben responded, "Shall be content alright, as content as a hungry wolf i' front of fresh dispatch."

Hamilton coughed softly. "General Washington, if I may add, I'm most impressed with the training. The men are being shaped, especially the militia that is with us. The British shall be in for quite a surprise when next they see us."

Washington rose from his chair, his face beamed with pride. "To be honest I was skeptical at first if the Baron would be able to pull this off, this difficult task, yet by the blessings of Providence he hath blessed us all." Hamilton translated for Steuben. Steuben's lips twinged as he fought back a smile that could not be resisted. It turned into a release of sunshine much better than the sun on this wintry day. Steuben faced Washington, his eyes squinting, giving the impression he was thinking hard to get the words out in English.

"It int all me. I reckon good lads primrose to shape because of their good approach and, General, you're the benison for us all." Steuben saluted followed by Hamilton.

"Gentlemen wouldst you like to share a cup of tea," said Washington.

Hamilton translated and exchanged a few words with Steuben. Hamilton exhaled softly. "If we may make haste, General, the Baron is needed."

"Of course, continue your good efforts gentlemen, join spring we attack the British and pay 'em back for any regress that needs accounting for."

Washington continued to work at his desk, alone with his thoughts. There were times when they were his rescuers but mostly now they were tormentors. His stomach shifted uneasily and subconsciously he found himself clenching his fist. Not for the first time he questioned whether he should have accepted command to defend the colonies. He was ambitious enough to take command for himself but not if it was the wrong decision for the men he led. His heart ached for his men and he felt responsible for them. Well. He thought. No turning back now. I shall not let the men down or the souls that hast thus departed. Dear Father, let it not be mine pride that hath chosen mine place yet by thy intervention.

As evening approached his stomach began to grumble and complain. He lost track of time and had refused all food offerings by his enslaved manservant, named Billy. At dinner time Billy insisted that he take a break and eat. Washington relented to Billy, mostly due to his becoming fond of the food prepared by a free black woman named Margaret Thomas from Philadelphia. Besides taking a liking to Billy, she had taken a liking to being a great cook and her food was loved by the revolutionary officers she cooked for. She could take ordinary and poor scraps and turn them into an amazing meal. Besides the delicious food, Martha would be returning soon to join him for the meal. Martha's presence always helped Washington's mood, especially if he was seized by a dark one.

Washington sat at a small wooden table waiting for Martha. His eyes lingered on a candle flickering on the table. Night approached. Billy laid out plenty of candles around the small room to fight off the darkness. Martha arrived just as the food was being served. Dinner consisted of a small piece of mutton, caramelized and cooked perfectly with roasted onion. Martha sat down just as Billy was pouring a glass of watered-down rum. Washington and Martha bowed their heads.

"Lord, bless this food we are about to receive," said Washington. He looked at Martha tenderly. "How was your visit to the hospital, dear? I'm sure it granted enjoyment to those poor souls." He spoke, taking a bite off his plate.

Martha's face lit up with excitement. "My affairs today were a matter of great excitement for me. I met a delightful young woman today, by the name of Mary, at one of the hospitals. Mary's care and attention to the men forsooth touched my heart. I doth wish I had some sort of ribbon or medal to grant out to discover our thanks. Something akin to what the Baron is aye wearing I suppose."

Washington looked up in thought. "I'm sure your presence was a reward for 'em, however, I suspect I may be able to do something. Next time, please collect their names so I may write a personal letter of thanks."

"Oh, I'm sure they will appreciate that," replied Martha.

"My dearest, I wish I could do more for 'em. Congress is of little help now, yet at least winter shall be ending anon and I shall be able to get 'em out of this purgatory at camp."

There was a disappointment on Martha's face. Just a tiny flicker. "The sooner we are out of hither the better. I wot thou shall doth all in your power for the men. You may underestimate how much your corporal presence means to 'em. A nod from you or a handshake is worth more than gold to 'em; it is the gift of hope. I shall compose another visit to the camp tomorrow and I desire you to accompany me if you art able."

"I shall accompany you tomorrow. Although I shall want to keep up late and finish my work. If you believe my corporal presence shall inspire 'em, so be it; who am I to argue with my better half? A happy wife is a fortunate life."

Martha looked pleased.

By the time Martha went to bed, Washington was still up, late into the night toiling over his writing of military affairs and politics. He fell asleep at his desk unable to stay awake. Billy, holding a candle, woke Washington with a gentle shake then led Washington to Washington's bedroom. Martha was gently snoring. He helped Washington change into his sleep shirt, then placed a flat metal warming-pan filled with hot coals between the sheets to keep the couple warm. Billy glanced at the couple briefly before exiting the bedroom. The spartan couple was a force to reckon with. He never met a couple like them, so devoted to each other and their love of others. He hummed a hymn as he walked to his bedroom:

> . . . . . *Yet, saith the Lord, He loves us so,*
> *He brought forth George to lead us all.*
> *His hands shall ruin'd the British walls,*
> *They shout his name 'i all the halls.*
> *An American Fabius hath been unleashed,*
> *to fight for liberty till its complete.*
> . . . . . *Yet, saith the Lord, He loves us so,*
> *He brought forth Martha to regard us all.*
> *Her love and generosity are a beacon for us,*
> *To pester her thou had been nuts*
> *A daughter of revolution hath been unleashed*
> *to fight for liberty till its complete.*

CHAPTER 10

DRILL SERGEANT

A fierce wind blew. A moment ago a loud crash had sounded like a tree branch crushed under the weight of snow on it. A lone Rhode Island Militiaman stood a few steps ahead of the front rank holding a lightly stained flag. The flag fluttered in the icy wind. This flag embraced a green pine tree image in the center with the words "An Appeal to Heaven" stitched above. Both the Revolutionaries and British pleaded for God's favor and intervention in this war but only one would ultimately have his favor.

Samuel Hollered, "Position of attention!" He tried to speak in a commanding voice but it came out in a croak. "M-Men." He cleared his throat. "We're gonna compose a cat's paw out of you. To act as soldiers you first might not but look like one." He paused for a moment as puffs of white vapor came out with his breath, owing to the cold air. "You have all been instructed what equipment to have with you. Let's see if you listen." Samuel continued trying to mimic what Baron Steuben would say. "When the musket balls are flying toward thee, it is too late to adjourn and fetch anything. Without proper equipment you let yourself down and the man beside you."

The review started with the flag bearer. This would be Samuel's first inspection and drill of troops after Baron Steuben released him from the model training company to train others. The young flag bearer, maybe 17, looked confident with a slight edge to his eyes, which said, Don't tread on me. Looking over the young lad, Samuel spotted a dark, stained wood pipe tucked behind a belt. Samuel frowned, then he grabbed the pipe and tossed it onto the snow-covered ground. The pipe sunk into the snow, almost completely buried. The flag bearer's head whipped around, eyes afire to look at his pipe. Samuel moved on quickly to his next prey. Remarkably, the next man had forgotten his ammunition box. "Are you going to throw mud balls or snow at the enemy?" The man's face turned a dark crimson. He was middle-aged with flecks of grey in his hair, with crow feat eyes that spoke of laughter in a previous life. No laughter now. "Well, maybe you can bayonet 'em to death instead if it's sharp enough." Samuel pulled out the militiamen's bayonet from its leather sheath and touched the tip. It drew a tiny speck of red. "Good, at least this is sharp." He re-sheathed the bayonet and continued his inspection, pointing out mistakes and tossing unnecessary equipment to sink in the snow.

Samuel found fault in every man but one. That lucky individual, Cato Bannister. Samuel looked and looked, but could not find any fault. Defeated in his efforts, he smiled. "Great job, Cato. If only your fellow patriots would follow your lead." Cato's face beamed with pride and he split a grin wide enough to show a missing tooth. "You passed today's inspection. Let's see if you can keep it up, Cato."

Cato's pride barely went down a notch. "Yes, sergeant."

Under a light snowfall, Samuel led the company around the field in marching maneuvers. Rome wasn't built in a day, and Samuel had his work cut out for himself. At the end of the day, he would have a better appreciation of the efforts it took for Baron Steuben to re-shape the army, like crafting stone into fine sculpture. When the men began to have a clue, which was a while, he marched them back to where the excess equipment was cast off earlier. Some personal items were now completely buried. Later, men would need to dig a little into the freezing snow to retrieve them. Alas, the flag bearer's pipe was never found again. I believe they will be more the wiser next time, he thought to himself. "All of thee still have a ways to go. We will practice until we have it correct. The flag bearer tried to mask a yawn. "If you feel you are tired, wait till tomorrow. We start again at first light. Now collect your stuff. Tomorrow, if I see anything not part of your uniform it may not be returned to you. Dismissed!"

Cato approached Samuel and blocked his path. He pulled out a paper from his pocket with a flourish and handed it to Samuel. "Did you see this, Samuel?" Samuel read it. Feb 14, 1778, The Rhode Island General Assembly hereby enable Every-bodied negro, mulatto, or Indian man to voluntarily enlist and earn freedom upon his passing muster of Colonel Christopher Green, be immediately discharged from the service of his master or mistress, and be absolutely free." Samuel's eyes lit up. "That's great tidings, Cato."

Cato spoke excitedly. "My master will be reimbursed by the Rhode Island Assembly. I will be a free man when this war is over. I have communicated patience in my indentured service, which is sensibly felt but now I have thought of new plans."

Samuel put his head down slightly. "Cato, let's talk more over some warmth. I need a fire before I freeze to death."

Cato nodded and followed Samuel to the nearest fire pit. They sat near the fire, the flames moving as the cold wind sent sparks everywhere.

"Have you given thought to what you may do for trade? I know Mr. Humphrey had thoughts in mind," said Samuel. Cato rubbed his hands as close to the fire without burning them. "I'm sure he does. I respect him, but I do not want to work in the mercantile field in Newport, that I know for sure. I will think about it plenty. I'm not going anywhere soon, that's the lot of it."

"Well, Cato, whatever you chose it will not be the Cato of ancient Rome." George Washington and the entire revolutionary generation all knew of the famous Roman Senator. Cato personified liberty. He was the last man standing when Rome's Republic fell. For Julius Caesar, the dictator who was famous for his mercy, Cato was the only man that he could never forgive.

Cato smiled. "I don't believe I'll have the favor to join the accord of Congress, but I wouldn't mind giving them a piece of my mind."

"About what, Cato?" Cato looked up to the sky in thought. His face looked full of intensity. He let out a long breath. "Would love to have a good blanket and a good meal."

Samuel chuckled. "Is that what you want? I thought you were about to give some sort of political speech."

"Samuel, I care not for politics. I do care about killing me a few red coats, though."

"As do I, Cato. As do I."

Twilight was fast approaching, the sky was darkening. Both men returned to their respective cabins, unable to endure the freezing temperature any longer. Samuel listened to the wind howl as it fought to get into the cabin. The steady sound lulled him to sleep.

CHAPTER 11

LOST CHILD

Cato brushed off the thick layer of straw he used in lieu of a blanket. Samuel had said he would be exhausted from the drills yesterday but as the light began to creep into the dark cabin, Cato had not gotten much sleep. His body was exhausted but his mind raced. His mind was set to pondering his freedom. Pondering his future. If he could survive this war his life would change forever. He decided to trudge along the camp to make sense of his muddled thoughts before drills.

Before he departed, Cato tossed in more wood into the cabin's pathetic, little fireplace that gave little warmth. His cabin mates would appreciate it. He was the only African American in the cabin. It mattered very little. Maybe a few remarks mostly jokes. All were brothers when the musket balls fired at them and when men suffered together. He opened the cloth flap door and stepped outside into the ankle-deep slushy mud. The cold stung him instantly. Not for the first time he wanted to pull off the door and wrap it around himself. Maybe hell is not an inferno but a never-ending ice storm. The camp roads were a quagmire of risk.

Cato focused on his steps carefully, trying not to slip in the icy ruts formed by the carts and wagon wheels. He pulled a cloth rag over his nose to deter the stench of gasses escaping from hundreds of horses buried in shallow graves.

Cato had very little memory of his homeland in Guinea, Africa. He remembered it as a tropical paradise, warm and humid. He did not remember much but he was positive it wasn't cold. He shivered. Many African Americans escaped to join the British. The Revolution was a war for independence and freedom. The irony was not lost on them. Cato joined due to the atrocities the British committed in this war. He heard nasty stories of British occupation. How the British Army looted and tortured their fellow men. In dreams, he watched the shelling of incendiary rounds into Falmouth, Massachusetts, and imagined the screams of the victims burning alive. Subsequently, the people of Falmouth were left to fend in winter without food. He was also a witness to the sound of a British navy ship that shelled the town of Bristol, Rhode Island after townspeople refused to deliver livestock to them. What irked Cato the most was the treatment of the American prisoners of war by the British. The defeated Americans were sometimes killed on the field crying out for mercy or taken to die on prison ships from the ravages of disease in cramped quarters. In his mind, King George had a lot to pay for and Cato wanted to deliver some payback.

At some point, the war would end. Cato was confident that the Rebels would win and he needed to puzzle in his head what to do after the war. It could be years, Cato understood, but it did not stop him from dreaming or obsessing about life after the war. He worked in Newport and Providence, Rhode Island. Both these cities were magnificent mercantile ports, so prosperous it made Rhode Island one of the wealthiest colonies. Little Rhody, as it was called, was the first to renounce King George, but the last to sign the constitution, not wanting to share its wealth with its neighboring colonies. Cato did not have many opinions about politics. He did not want to go back after the war and continue his indentured trade. He thought his best opportunity would be as a cabbage farmer, that is, if he could acquire enough money and land. He believed farming was a noble profession and in the worst case, he would never go hungry. With his earnings as a soldier maybe he could make a start. His friend Samuel would offer some advice. Deep in thought, Cato continued walking, oblivious to his dangerous surroundings.

A clap of hooves from a galloping horse sounded. Cato jumped just in time and landed in slushy filth. Well, he was not exactly sure what it was, but it smelled something fierce. He was wiping the muck off himself when he abruptly stopped in his tracks. A young child, maybe age 4, stood behind a cabin and was sobbing. Cato glanced around looking for the child's family, but no one was around. He moved to help the boy. The boy had tousled light brown hair that badly needed to be combed. He was dressed in ragged clothes that stunk. "Boy, who is watching over ye?" The boy, with tears in his eyes, only shrugged.

"Well, we need to find who is in charge of ye?" Cato fumbled into his pocket pulling out a small crust of bread he saved from last night's meal. He handed the bread to the boy. The boy ate it and his tears began to vanish. "What is your name, child?"

"N-Na---Nathaniel, sir"

"What a sweet name, now do tell me where your parents are or who has a charge over ye?"

"Father's dead and I'm lost." The boy looked about to cry again. "I was looking at a horse. I named him Sami. I wanted to play a knight so I went to hunt sticks. Then mother was gone."

"Well, let's remedy that, shall we—hhmm, what is her name?"

The boys' eyes brightened. "Mother," he replied.

Cato frowned. "What's your name again, little one?"

"Nathaniel."

"Well, Nathaniel, it's freezing here. Let's be on our way to the camp followers' camp. Someone is bound to recognize you."

The boy looked at Cato, puzzled for a moment, then pointed up at him. "Why are you so dirty." Cato heard this before from young white children that did not know any better.

"That's the color of my skin and it doesn't wash off." Cato smiled. "That is how God made me. Do you know about God?" The boy nodded. "Well, just remember he loves us all regardless of color. We all are the children of God. Now let's find ye folks."

Cato took the child by the hand and walked to the camp followers bivouac area. Once in the camp, it did not take long for Nathaniel to be recognized. "Nathaniel, is that you?" a young boy about 11 asked; he looked like Nathaniel's larger twin. Nathaniel almost leaped in the air then charged the boy giving him a bear hug.

The 11-year-old looked directly at Cato. "My name is Thomas, Thank you, sir, for leading him back to camp. Mother is in a desperate way. Father died of illness a few days ago, I don't reckon she can take anymore bad news."

Cato ruffled Nathaniel's hair. "Don't mention it. Go and get him to his mother in due haste."

Thomas grabbed Nathaniel's hand. "Let's go, Nathaniel before mother dies of fright."

Nathaniel ripped his hand from Thomas then went over to Cato and gave him a big hug. Cato received his payment for the boy's return and it was more valuable than any gold on earth.

CHAPTER 12

DAWN OF SPRING

Before Samuel entered, he tried his best to stomp off the muddy sludge that built upon his shoes. Inside the cabin, a Constitutional Postman was holding a short stack of letters tied with a string, pulled from a bulky sack. "If thou would pardon, sergeant, I hast letters to deliver to this cabin. May you please check to make sure the addressees reside here. I'd hate to deliver to the wrong place." Samuel broke the string and shuffled through the letters quickly. He smiled when he came across a letter from his brother Duncan.

"You've found the right seat here, my friend."

The postman hoisted his bag to his shoulder. "Good to hark this. Blessed day to you, sergeant."

Samuel still had a few minutes till his new duties as a sergeant placed him leading a small foraging expedition. In this detail, he was able to pick any two Continentals soldiers to assist. He chose William Anthony, called Bill, the one in his cabin with the perpetual scowl. Samuel couldn't decide on any soldier that needed more fresh air. His final pick was Joseph Martin, who had previously helped Samuel cart the ill. He believed Joseph would be grateful to get out of camp and at least hauling supplies would be more appealing than hauling the sick to the hospital.

More and more pleasant days were coming, which helped place the camp in a better mood, even though the warming sun did turn campgrounds soggy. March was the start of a list of blessings. Early in the month, the incompetent quartermaster Thomas Mifflin, whom Washington was deeply disappointed in, was replaced by General Nathaniel Greene. Born into a wealthy Quaker family from Warwick, Rhode Island, he was one of Washington's most capable military officers. Greene would continue to lead men into battle when the drums called, but for now, he set to work on fixing the supply issues. He rapidly dispatched engineers to improve roads and bridges to Valley Forge. Wagons finally began arriving with needed supplies of food and clothing. A further blessing in early March was the arrival of a baking company led by German-born Christopher Ludwig. The Philadelphia baker brought 70 men to camp to finally fulfill the promise by Congress that each soldier would receive their daily pound of bread. Soldiers' stomachs profited from the bread but Ludwig, a true patriot, refused compensation from his labor. Yes, March was a blessing, topped off by Washington giving each soldier an extra month's pay for remaining steadfast during the miseries of winter. To further raise spirits he gave each soldier a ration of rum.

Samuel sat down near the fireplace to read the letter from Duncan. The folded letter was dated January 20th, 1778, and marked "On Publick Service," a typical marking for military mail sent for free through the Constitutional Post. During wartime, soldiers could have their personal mail sent for free, as long as it was marked by an officer in charge. Samuel eagerly opened the letter. The letter had a good many crease lines but was readable.

Dear Brother,

Since Newport tis under British control, I do not know how Mother and Father fare. The British have it locked down well. Since the Gaspee Affair—after that British Customs Schooner be sunk. The British Schooners have been patrolling Narragansett Bay and raiding coastal towns and islands indiscriminately, grabbing livestock and goods. We struggle with not enough militia to patrol the coast.

We defended Prudence Island after the woman and children were removed. The British had the gall to tell us they would arrive on January 12, 1776, thinking to avoid a skirmish. Samuel Pearce of the 2nd Portsmouth Company told them, redcoats, that they would get nothing but a bayonet point. I was with the fifty men dug in to defend. Unfortunately, we were outnumbered and 250 Royal Marines sent us in retreat, but on the next day reinforcements arrived and they retreated to their ships.

We did plan a secret attack to take Newport with the Massachusetts and Connecticut Militia joining us, but when the day came to attack a heavy gale blew preventing the assault. The British got wind of the assault and the invasion is now called off. I pray for victory, be it God's will, and that we meet again soon.

Your dear brother.

Duncan Fox

First checking to make sure there was no hole in his well-worn coat pocket, Samuel folded the letter carefully and placed it in his coat. Bill and Joseph entered the cabin together. Joseph immediately noticed the red cloth stitched to Samuel's coat. "Congratulations, sergeant, that looks good on you." Samuel smiled and touched the red cloth with his finger absently. Joseph continued, "Thank you, sergeant, for choosing me for this detail. It will surely be good to stretch my legs out and my nose would love a good helping of fresh air after the foul odors of camp." Bill said nothing, simply nodded, but his scowl did not appear as deep today. Samuel gave out a deep breath. "Well, men, let's get to it. I could use a refreshing change of scenery, believe you me."

Samuel reviewed their duty assignment with Bill and Joseph. They were to go foraging for spruce buds. The tender spruce buds were just emerging from their brown, papery husks. The tips were needed for many uses. They could be added to soups, baked into cookies and bread, and of course, used in spruce beer. The task was to go out and harvest as much as they could collect before dark and bring the harvest to the supply depot at camp.

The men signed out horses to help carry the large load they anticipated, each receiving a young chestnut mare in surprisingly good health. They packed lightly, a few biscuits for a meal, and each took a pair of large empty sacks. Weapons would be taken. Each took their long gun musket and Samuel placed his pistol under his belt. There was always a possibility of running into a British scout but the odds were rather slim. As the saying goes, best to have weapons and not need them than to need them and not have them.

They traveled along dirt roads past farms and pastures that covered most of the land outside Valley forge. Far from the dirt roads that led to camp, they detoured into the nearest forest to begin the harvest. No forest hum of life greeted them, only the sound of cracking twigs and leaves underfoot the horses. Soon spring would come with sounds of life, including birds that sang sweetly, but not today. The forest greeted them with the smell of dead leaves and moist earth that filled the forest with a scent that seemed not to belong to this earth.

The men set to work, picking the tender buds carefully to prevent overharvesting. Too much plucking could damage and even kill a tree. Take only what you need, his mother taught him. The men tried to keep close together, but gradually they separated just out of sight of each other. In the beginning, Samuel called the men to make sure they were in earshot, but his calls to them now became fewer and fewer. He had not called in over an hour, so focused on the task at hand. His first sack was now half full. If the others were having as much success, they would easily finish filling all the sacks before dark.

Samuel guided his horse to the next tree with promising new buds. He tied his mare to a low-hanging branch on a nearby oak tree. He placed his musket on the spruce trunk and grabbed his sack to start at the far side of the tree. He wiped the sweat from his brow then took a sip from his canteen. Reaching for a tender bud he heard the distinctive sound of a flintlock pulled back. Turning to face the sound he imagined a British scout in his red coat, instead, it was a filthily dressed farmer missing a noticeable amount of teeth and aiming a muzzle-loaded long gun at him. Two similarly dressed men, somewhere in their middle years with faces unremarkable, stood on either side of the toothless man, their long gun muskets aimed at Samuel as well. The group's action struck Samuel like a blow to his stomach, his eyes started half out of his head, and his mouth worked soundlessly. Darn, I should have brought a pass with me. Too late now. He recovered quick enough and gazed at his loaded musket resting against a tree. He clenched his fist in frustration. "Ow don,t ye move!" the toothless man spluttered. "We get a larger bounty for deserters"—a short pause—"alive 'tis."

Samuel glared up at the man's toothless grin and swallowed hard. "I can assure you, I am out foraging spruce for camp."

He was cut off by Toothless. "Ye mean gathering food for your long trip back home." Samuel regretted his musket was out of reach and especially losing sight of Joseph and Bill. He was tempted to yell out for help or pull out his pistol but thought better of it. Instead, he talked as loud as he could without shouting, hoping his men would hear him.

"You can drag me back to camp, but no bounty will be collected for me. I assure you!" Samuel pleaded hoarsely.

"That's what they all say, isn't that right, Thomas?" Toothless turned to the man on his left.

Thomas answered, "You bet. They say anything to keep a noose from their necks."

Toothless snickered. "Tie 'em up, boys." Samuel's heart pounded through his ribs as anger roared inside himself about to burst into an explosion. His eyes narrowed to notches, staring at Toothless.

"Gentlemen," a loud voice called out from some thick brush. Samuel heard the voice of Bill. "If you would kindly drop your weapons, please." The farmers could not see Bill but turned in the direction of his voice. They appeared a little deaf, from the way they tilted their heads to catch Bill's voice better. Out walked Bill, totally fearless, his musket aimed at the leader of the motley crew. Samuel took that moment to take out his pistol, cock it, and aimed directly at the leader's head, close range. Toothless swung, bulging eyes going from Samuel to Bill and back, slowly widening until the whites showed all the way around.

"Drop 'em, boys." The farmers dropped their weapons slowly to the ground. Samuel grabbed the weapons and quickly tossed them far out of reach into knee-high brown grass. At that moment Joseph arrived riding his horse. Quickly, he grabbed his musket attached to the saddle and surveyed the scene with those deep brown pools of his eyes.

"They are definitely not red coats," Joseph smirked. "Looking at their frowns, they look more like deserters of Robin Hood's merry band of men. Shucks, I can't believe I missed all the fun." Samuel gave a short chuckle. Bill suddenly doubled himself over and burst into a loud harsh cackle of laughter. It was the sound of someone that hadn't laughed in a thousand years. Samuel hoped that it would be enough to erase Bill's scowl forever.

"Oh, that's a good one, Joseph. Robin Hood's merry men," Bill spit out. "They were hunting their prey, now their prey is about to turn the tides on 'em. Not fine hunters indeed, methinks. Thou mess with wolf thou get all of the pack."

Samuel delivered a tongue lashing on the subject of manners that left the crew of bounty hunters spluttering indignantly. The toothless leader begrudgingly gave his name as Benedict and apologized over and over again as smooth as butter, but it did not appear genuine enough for Samuel. Samuel thought for a moment then spoke. "Gentlemen? I figure your successful bounty hunters. I'm sure you would love to leave a donation for camp for the misunderstanding. Frankly, I must insist."

Benedict frowned. "I have some good Virginian tobac here. Take it." Benedict's frown seemed genuine now as he tossed a small but stuffed bag from under his coat.

The bounty hunters collected their weapons with defeated looks. Each of them glanced back in sullen resentment, as they returned into the forest. Promptly, Samuel's detail returned to their task. They lost valuable time with the interruption, but they were able to fill all the sacks prior to leaving the forest. They stuck together this time in eyesight of each other and when finished rode out closely together. Riding out, Samuel took the time to thank Bill. If Bill had not been there, they may all have been dragged back to Valley Forge and never able to live down the embarrassment. Bill's chest swelled with pride. "To be honest with you, Samuel, I felt tempted to desert myself from time to time. I've been miserable hither because I miss mine wife. Mine wife passed away a few months since. It hath been hard to bear. Mine farm bids me like the sounds of the sirens bidding, yet I shall not walk out on mine brothers" His voice was a touch breathy and shrill yet proud. "Till I be out of ammo or out of blood." His perpetual scowl vanished never to return.

CHAPTER 13

DAVID AND GOLIATH

Jacob was in a deep sleep. He stepped lightly following the barely noticeable deer track. He tried to slow his heart rate as he approached a magnificent stag. It was a truly majestic animal, proudly standing with the most beautiful horns he had ever seen. He cocked the hammer on his musket, aimed, and fired. A puff of black smoke spread through the air. Jacob ran towards the deer. It struggled to move, kicking its legs slowly. Taking his knife, he silenced the stag forever. Sitting with his legs under him, Jacob gave a quick prayer of thanks. He then placed his prize over his shoulder and followed the familiar path home.

Jacob heard loud voices arguing and ducked into the overgrown foliage to see what the fuss was. He looked up through an opening in the brush and he stared at a colonist arguing with a British soldier. The colonist was dressed like a typical militiaman and the British soldier wore a sharp, blood-red uniform. Suddenly, the colonist sputtered something inaudible, his eyes went wide. He took out a pistol from his belt and shot the British soldier square in the chest. The soldier cursed barely discernible as his life faded quickly away.

The colonist dropped the pistol to the ground. A Native American suddenly appeared walking towards the colonist. The native wore a large smile. He was dressed in traditional leather deerskins that Jacob had not seen in some time. The native was steps away from the colonist. The colonist embraced the native then pulled out a pistol from behind his breeches, pointed the muzzle to the native's heart, and shot. The Native American sputtered, "W-Why!"

Jacob woke wide awake, his heart pounded, mind empty, as if he was being chased by a mother grizzly bear protecting her young. He strained to see into the early morning light, as his breathing rate began to steady. Out of bed, he splashed cold water on his face. The act did nothing to wash away his strange dream. With no appetite, he skipped breakfast, dressed, then went outside to watch the first light.

Jacob watched the spreading sunrise, oranges, and reds painted across the clouds announcing the new day. A distant dog barked and another answered. He decided to walk. With no direction at first, he made his way to the Oneida Stone. Approaching the stone he met Han Yerry – Tewahongalahkon ("He Who Takes Up the Snowshoe"), a member of the Wolf Clan and a good friend. Han was a sachem who lived at Oriska but recently moved to Kanonwalohale. Oriska and parts of the Oneida were more pagan and did not have as much support for the colonists. Han decided it was more comfortable to live in Kanonwalohale. He was an impressive, muscular warrior just a tad shorter than his friend John. His head was shaved with only a long crest of dark brown hair down the center of his head with splayed feathers.

Jacob turned to the warrior. "How is wife and son, and your wrist?" A musket ball went through Hans' wrist at the Battle of Oriskany, August 6, 1777. Han's spouse, "Two Kettles Together" (Tyonajanegen), and his son Cornelius also fought bravely at Oriskany; when Han was wounded, his wife loaded his gun for him so he could continue his deadly shooting.

"The wrist is good, my friend, and my family, but I see in your eyes you have more on your mind than my wrist healing. I set my heart upon knowing why."

"I had the most vivid dream last night. I can't tell you why the dream bothers me so, I cannot even think about it without my stomach twisting. I feel somehow there is a message in this dream. I feel it has something to do with us supporting the colonists. Do we make a good choice to split the Confederacy over another nation's civil war and enter the conflict?"

Han paused for a moment contemplating. He brushed his hand over his bald head. His eyes fixed on Jacob. "Do you remember the great Peacemaker, Deganawidah, also had a dream or vision similar to yours. He prophesied that a 'white serpent' would join a new people's lands and compose friends with 'em, only to mock 'em later. A 'red serpent' would later compose war against the 'white serpent' and after a time a 'black serpent' would later defeat both the 'white' and 'red serpents.'" Jacob pressed his hand against his temple and listened. "According to prophecy, when the people gathered under the elm tree they were humbled, all three 'serpents' blinded by a light many times more brilliant than the sun. Deganawidah said that the 'red serpent' wouldst accept the 'white serpent' into their safekeeping as a long-lost brother. I think perhaps the colonists are maybe the 'white serpent,' the British Empire the 'red serpent' and the Native Americans the 'black serpent.' I believe that the almighty God will lead us towards a path for good reason. The Bible tells us we are sheep and we will be led to green pastures and still waters. I have faith that it will all work out in the end. I feel deep down that as a people we shall be stronger at the end of this conflict."

Jacob mulled on Han's words. He pressed his hand against his temple as he pondered Han's revelation. He looked up at the sky and glimpsed two small birds angrily protecting a nest from a large black crow. "I hope you are right, my friend. The Bible does tell us he will set a table for us in the midst of our enemies, whoever they are. I believe you speak the truth and you have eased my mind, along with my heart. I will keep faith that it will work out in the end."

"Dine with me and my family tonight, my friend. We'd be honored to hast thy company. My son caught a plump turkey early this morning. He has almost bettered me as a hunter. Although I prefer you to keep that between us. Well, what do you say? Will you help us to finish it?"

Jacob clasped Han's soldier. "It is I that shall be honored. Count me in."

With his stomach now growling, Jacob would head back home to eat. Before he departed he looked up to the sky. The crow had gone, most likely beaten off by the two small birds less than half its size. The determination of many committed to a common cause can accomplish anything. The message would be coming shortly with Chief Shenendoah's return to Kanonwalohale: the final account of what direction the Oneida would take in the colonists' war for independence.

Jacob could not help but think of the war as pitting Goliath, "The British," against David, "The Colonists," only this time Goliath had all the weapons and ammunition. This would be no old-fashioned battle with the young men of the enemy coming to fight the young men that would die to protect their homeland, both with similar means at their disposal. The British like most of Europe was ruled by monarchs and nobles who brutalized and subdued the population, in the name of the law and taxation, so they could foster great military strength to bear on their enemies. How could the colonists resist such long-standing power? Jacob was rooting for David, although he could not see David winning. Like the real David in the Bible, the colonists needed a miracle.

CHAPTER 14

GRANT ME SERENITY

Polly hacked at the soil with her hoe as she worked around a stubborn rock. Dirt flew into the air. She remembered her mother telling her in the northern soil of this great continent it would be easier to harvest stones than crops. She repeated the process letting out her frustration about the pending war for her people with every stubborn rock she unearthed.

Whack--the blade dislodged a wedge of gray stone.

It all depended on the decision of the clan mothers and Chief Shenendoah. The clans of the Oneida—the turtle, wolf, and bear clans—could soon be at war! Her people's peaceful ways could be changed forever. For the sake of taking sides in a war between one group of white men and another. What have the white men brought us? Pain? Suffering? My people forget their past and the roots they have planted. Besides decimating native populations with diseases, the land-hungry colonists continue to push us into warfare. When the confederacy formed, we buried our weapons under the roots of the white pine with a promise of peace. We have lived united for generations. This peace must not be broken. It must not!

With a frustrated sigh, she picked up the stone. The strain made her hunch as she carried it to the partially built wall and placed it carefully upon the others. She saw Good Peter approaching. She wiped the sweat off her brow, leaving a clean streak on her filthy face, and padded the dirt smeared across her clothes.

"Good day and peace to you," said Peter.

She crossed her arms, one hand still gripping the hoe. "What brings you here, preacher?"

"Out for a walk."

Polly tugged one of her braids. It made her two braids become loose. "Simply out for a stroll. Really?"

"Truthfully, I came to talk to you."

Polly raised an eyebrow. "About what?"

After a quick, amused smile, Peter said. "I will cut to the chase. You will be a clan mother one day, and you will make your people proud, but I worry you take on too much of the burden of the nation upon yourself. You must remember you are only one. A well-known prayer is often spoken, 'God, grant me the serenity to accept the things I cannot change, the courage to change the things I can, and wisdom to know the difference.' You must learn to cast your troubles on God. His love for us runs deep. He will help you. He will help our people. If we depend on him and walk with him." This last was said with the lilt of a question in Peter's voice. Polly did not take the hint. "How is your walk with the Lord?"

Polly tugged uncomfortably at her braid. "I pray, but he does not listen or he chooses to ignore me."

"He listens, but answers in his way and time. His thoughts are greater than ours. He is the Shepherd, and we are the sheep. He answers our prayers often. We must listen to his voice, and he will guide us."

Polly absently kicked a stone on the ground. She had to admit that she was not the kind to sit patiently and wait for directions.

"Always bear in mind that you must involve God in all things. In doing so we may better serve him and our fellow neighbors," Peter said.

Polly drew herself up as much as she could, which was not very far since she was inches shorter than Peter. Her face was a mask of serenity. "I shall try and remember your counsel. Good day to you."

Polly waited.

"Well, I hope that you do Polly. I truly do."

Another fleeting smile on Peter's face.

What's he smiling at? Polly thought, with a hint of irritation.

With a slight dip of his head, Peter said, "Good day to you," and turned and walked away.

Polly watched him for several moments. He was a good spirit and would do anything for his people. She could not help but respect the former warrior, and could not doubt his genuine faith in the Great Father and his Son, but Polly did not find trust easy. A warrior who has found peace. For now. She pulled her braid again as she walked back to remove stones.

CHAPTER 15
SACRIFICE OF THE ONEIDA

The sun shone brightly among the fluffy clouds that dotted the blue sky. The scene would have only been more picturesque if painted. A gentle breeze kept the heat of the sun at bay. It was a perfect day to welcome the Great Chief Shenendoah back to his home at Kanonwalohale. A good day to find out the direction of the Oneida nation with the conference concluded with the colonists.

Jacob stood with a large crowd of Oneida, circled around Chief Shenendoah just inside the wooden palisade at Kanonwalohale. A small group of men wearing mostly continental uniforms mixed in with a few French uniforms stood nearby the chief's right side. To his left was an equal-sized group of Clan Mothers. The proud chief stood in full regalia. He wore a traditional headdress, a feathered cap that had two feathers straight up and one down, differentiating the Oneida from other tribes of the Confederacy, and a beautiful braided leather necklace that displayed large bear claws around his neck. More distinguishing than his regalia was his face. The lines on his face etched the story of a hard life for the great leader. His eyes were those of a man who had lost what he knew he must lose, but that the knowledge did not soften them.

Shenendoah addressed the crowd with a loud voice that echoed against the silence of the crowd waiting in anticipation for his words. "Based upon the seventh generation to come it is agreed we will fight the British. The Oneida, joined by the Tuscaroras, will be the only members of the Haudenosaunee Confederacy to side with the colonists; we do this primarily because the rebel colonists are fellow neighbors and our Christian brothers. What would our brother Samuel Kirkland say if we did not help them? We live under a law of peace where many generations ago weapons of war were buried under a white pine, but now we must lift up our weapons. We must not ignore our Christian duty. We will be rewarded for our efforts. Showing kindness to a neighbor is a gift that is always returned. This nation has pledged scouts to aid the colonists. In return, they will help garrison and build a fort here at Kanonwalohale, protecting us, for we have been made a bullseye by the other tribes of the Confederacy. It is truly a matter of time before the British attack us and our allies, especially should our warriors be off fighting. Allow me now to introduce to you the Marquis de Lafayette."

A young man in a clean, new Continental uniform stepped to the side of Shenendoah. He looked almost too young to shave but he was clearly in command. An intensity in his brown eyes showed intelligence well beyond his years. In a thick French accent, the Marquis de Lafayette spoke: "George Washington, commander of the Continental Army, would like to offer his praise to your people. Your warriors had repeatedly proved themselves as exceptional scouts, and superb fighters. The Oneidas and Tuscaroras have a particular claim to attention and kindness, for their perseverance and fidelity." Lafayette paused for a moment and looked around the crowd, his deep brown pools staring through them. "For myself, it is not without trouble I have made this rapid march to you. I welcome your needed help with pleasure and call you friends." He nodded to the Chief then shook his hand. They both stared into each other's eyes, almost nose to nose, grateful but unsure of the alliance's success.

After Shenendoah dismissed the crowd, he gave instructions for the tribe's warriors and sachems to gather with him at dusk then he gathered his guests to show them polite hospitality. A tall warrior blocked Jacob's path. It was his friend John, a sachem from the Turtle Clan. Jacob smiled, "You now have your answer. Was it what you wanted to hear?"

John did not return the smile but frowned. "I was eager to fight." He reached down and picked up a small stone then tossed it. "But now I wonder if it makes sense to fight again in a white man's war. My father told me what Seneca Chief Tanaghrisson said during the war with the French. 'Both you and the English are white, we live in a country between; therefore the land belongs to neither one nor t'other: but the Great Being above allow'd it to be a place of residence for us; so fathers, I desire you to withdraw, as I have done our brothers the English; for I will keep you at arm's length: I lay this down as a trial for both, to see which will have the greatest regard to it, and that Side we will stand by, and make equal sharers with us. Our brothers the English have heard this, and I come now to tell it to you, for I am not afraid to discharge you off this land." John looked more sullen than Jacob had ever seen him. Jacob, unsure what to say, simply nodded in acknowledgment. John quickly forced a smile. "Looks like I won't be beating ye again in Lacrosse for a while at least."

Jacob chuckled. "You were lucky, my friend. It is better to have less thunder in the mouth and more lightning in the hand. Next time we play, if fortune pricks me, my team will win."

John cleared his throat. "If there is a next time."

The wooden meeting house was overcrowded with every warrior fit to fight and Sachem. The body heat was enough for sweat to trickle down everyone's face. Large candles cast a flickering light more than enough to illuminate the room. Chief Shenendoah wasted no time addressing the assembly. "Washington asked for two thousand warriors, nearly every able-bodied man to support the colonists' cause for independence. Lafayette has given us belts and gold coins as friendship inducements and has agreed to build a protective fort here. He has also promised us we will serve under French instead of colonial commanders. Two thousand warriors are impossible to send. Fort Schuyler is now in the colonists' hands; even though this stronghold is built on our land it is not close enough to protect us." His voice softened slightly. "Without better defenses, Kanonwalohale is vulnerable. Timbers are already being cut and Lafayette has called for French military engineers to assist. Tools and support from Fort Schuyler are en route. We offered them forty-nine warriors to serve as scouts." His shoulders slumped and he sighed. "They are not happy but have accepted our offer. The offer is better than those who have one foot in the canoe, and one foot in the boat, and are going to fall into the river."

A quick knock at the door and Polly Cooper stepped in. She turned to face Shenendoah. Her eyes were like a hawk focused on a target. "Clan mothers have inventoried and the council of elders agrees we shall bring 600 bushels of white corn to our starving brothers. I will be joining you to assist in the distribution."

All eyes turned on Polly. Shenendoah snapped his mouth so hard his teeth clicked. "This is a military trip," he said, "You cannot join us."

Color flared on her cheeks for just a moment. Polly's eyes fixed on her chief and she drew a deep breath. She placed her hands on her hips. In a calm voice, she spoke delicately, as delicate as a stone post: "The council insists."

A muscle in Shenendoah's face jumped at her tone, and he swallowed. Shenendoah scrubbed his hands through his hair, then pressed them hard against his temples. He lowered his head staring directly at Polly. "Agreed."

Polly held back a smug look and quickly exited the room.

"It is settled." Chief Shenendoah drew himself up. "Forty-nine warriors and one Polly Cooper will leave tomorrow accompanied by the Frenchman, Chevalier Tousard, a friend of the Marquis de Lafayette, to Valley Forge. Shenendoah then went around the room and handpicked the warriors for the mission. Jacob would be part of the 49 along with John, Daniel, one of the chief's sons, and Han Yerry. Shenendoah dismissed the group to get what rest they could before tomorrow's journey.

Washington would get his warriors as his loyal friend Lafayette had vowed to Washington to 'Undo to thy excellency some scalping gentlemen for dressing the brave air of the Howe.' Besides scouts, they would also deliver valuable corn to Washington's forces. Civilization owes much to corn and the early people who cultivated it. This plant, a common food today, appeared approximately 9,000 years ago. Native Americans used genetics much sooner than in ancient Greece. They took a Mexican grass called teosinte with a hard kernel that could easily break a tooth and turned it into a crop that was a giver of life blessed by God.

* * *

The Native American support was a blessing for the revolution. Lafayette only hoped they could deliver their part of the bargain. He knew most agreements with Native Americans, although begun on an honorable footing, seldom lasted long.

An Oneida Turtle Clan sachem named Odatseghte (Head Sachem) gave a heartfelt speech just prior to departure to Valley Forge. He implored the warriors and one Polly Cooper to make the Oneida Nation proud. "Thy souls are forever imprinted onto the stones of the Oneida Nation hie forth and compose your fathers and mothers proud."

The warriors hollered and cried out in unison, "Oonah, oonah." The Oneida would give up the protection of the Confederacy and risk their lives to aid the rebel colonists. Only time would tell if the sacrifice would be worth it.

---

[1]Tanaghrisson to the commander of a French fort, as reported to and recorded by George Washington, 25 November 1753, The Journal of Major George Washington (1754)

CHAPTER 16

DELIVERANCE

The Oneida allies and a small party of Lafayette's men set a fast pace through the woods. The midday sun casts a scattered light within the trees, mostly oak, sycamore, and dogwood. The earth was filled with a revival of dry browns turning to green foliage and burgeoning treetops. Timber was scattered everywhere, apparently from a windstorm years ago, making the ground difficult to navigate.

"Gollumpus," Jacob mumbled. His foot caught a root and he nearly slipped. His hand went to the middle of his back.

"Ye alright there?" Daniel said. "Just think of the hill climb as a lacrosse match with opponents trying to trip ye."

"Hark, my friend, have you got a padlock for thy mouth." Jacob lowered the sack of corn he carried to the ground and paused to catch his breath. He felt a hand gently touch his back.

It was Polly's hand, and she had a concerned look in her eyes. "I have a tincture of horsemint that will help with your discomfort."

"I'm fine. Just a little twist of my back."

"Give it over," said Polly as she pointed at Jacob's canteen. A murmur of assent from Jacob. "Good."

Jacob handed over his canteen and Polly added drops of her horsemint remedy. Jacob took a large swallow. The taste was bitter and smelled a little like thyme. He feigned a smile.

"Thu-thank You."

Daniel flashed a hand signal to Jacob. Jacob flashed it to Polly. Word had come from their spotter that a sentry from Valley Forge had been located. The party moved into the cover of the forest so as not to startle the sentry into mistaking them for hostiles. Frenchman Chevalier Tousard moved forward to parley with the sentry. In a few minutes, laughter could be heard. The all-clear signal was given. The march continued.

On May 15th, 1778, after trudging the entire 300-plus miles from upstate New York, the vigorous procession of Oneida warriors and one woman, Polly, strode into camp where the Rebel Army had endured great hardship during the previous winter. They were led out directly to General Washington's headquarters. There, the commander in chief greeted them with a great convention. The leaders dined with Washington and he gave them a belt, thankful for their help in the struggle for liberty. The Oneida warriors were assigned cabin space and Polly was given a small tent of her own.

On May 18th the newly arrived Native American allies would participate in a reconnaissance force, consisting of 2 brigades, about 2,200 men, under the command of Marquis de Lafayette; their objective was a position on Barren Hill. Samuel's brigade was one of the Continental brigades chosen to participate. Although the chosen would have a scant few days to prepare, they were excited to be on the march again. No more endless days of drills and boredom, they would take to the field and put their new training to the test. Once prey for the British, the Baron Steuben had transformed them into predators.

The wintertime had passed. Cold days at Valley Forge were ending and new energy abounded. Warm spring sunlight illuminated the fresh green growth. Along with a new season, good news appeared to boost morale and raise drowning spirits. The prayers lifted to God over the long months were finally being answered. The Schuylkill River nearby was teeming with shad that surged up the river to spawn. Soldiers stuffed themselves on the shad and hundreds of barrels were filled with salted shad for future use. The men's fingers dripped oil and the camp stunk of fish. Besides the blessing of fish, more farmers began bringing more crops to the camp market. More importantly, France had just entered the war as an ally of the new nation. A day of thanksgiving and great festivities were to be held in a camp on May 5, along with parading, gun salutes, and prayer.

Fresh military units were beginning to trickle in. Through necessity, the American army was moving from dependency on the landowner-run militia to enlistments of people who were newly woven into the fabric of the emerging nation. Mid Atlantic states were enrolling mostly foreign-born men from German, Irish, Scottish, and English immigrants who had poured in over the past ten years. So poor was recruitment in the beginning that many states instituted conscription and Congress approved generous bounties to fill the army's ranks. The town of Concord, Massachusetts, that of the famous minutemen, was reduced to rounding up free slaves and poor men with little job prospects to substitute for those who had lost their passion for joining the army. Hundreds of Native Americans enlisted in the Continental Army, such as the Stockbridge and Mohican Indians; they joined several New England regiments from Massachusetts and Connecticut.

Although still a teenager, Lafayette somehow convinced the Continental Army to commission him as a major general less than a year ago, though he spoke little English and lacked any battle experience. His first military action was at the Battle of Brandywine, near Philadelphia, on September 11, 1777, where Lafayette was shot in the calf. He impressed Washington by bravely refusing treatment so that he could lead a successful retreat. Lafayette was a fiercely loyal aide to Washington and wanted nothing more than to prove his worth to him. This would be the first major command of Lafayette, who had now turned twenty, handed to him by Washington.

After calling the chosen brigades for assembly and review, Lafayette released them. Samuel sat down and stretched his legs before a freshly lit campfire. Campfires were scattered in haphazard clumps of five or six friends around a fire. He sat on the ground watching the dancing orange and yellow flames leap hungrily for fuel. He added a stick to the fire and watched the flames leap and hiss. As he absorbed himself in the crackling and the woody fragrance of smoke, he gave way to his thoughts. We may have been tracked to Valley Forge with the blood of our feet, but we will be marching out stronger than when we entered. The Brits are surely in for a surprise from the brothers of liberty. He watched the dark smoke float through the air. His stomach growled. The chosen brigades were promised full bellies before departure.

The two brigades tasked for reconnaissance waited impatiently for corn to be distributed from the supply the Oneida brought to camp. When the corn arrived they tried to eat it raw but they struggled pitifully. Samuel spit out a good amount of precious food. He was disgusted it would go to waste. The white corn of the Oneida was unlike the yellow corn the soldiers knew. Its taste was unpleasant and the men had trouble digesting it. It didn't take long for the Oneida in camp to hear about it. The brigade was ordered not to throw the food away and told that a representative from the tribe would arrive shortly and teach the men how to prepare the corn properly.

A beautiful Native American woman appeared before the men. Her perfect skin and slender frame looked so fragile but not her eyes. Her brown eyes radiated intelligence and she moved with confidence in a long skirt decorated with beautiful multi-colored beads. Samuel's heart skipped a beat. She stared at Samuel with one eyebrow raised as she contemplated how to pronounce in English. "My name is Polly

Cooper. I welcome you. Do not eat corn raw. Let me show you how to prepare. Do you have pots?" Samuel dashed off quickly, returning with two large pots. "Now fill with water halfway." The water was added. "Good." She took a few heads of corn that she peeled from the husks and put them into the pot. She found some red-hot coals and set the pots on top of them. "Now keep corn in water till water bubbles a time." She sat till the corn was cooked then removed the cobs with a knife. When the corn cobs were cool, she passed them out. This time the corn tasted like a gift from heaven.

Polly sat on the ground and remained to watch the men eat the corn in all sorts of ways. Longways, vertically, from the middle and cutting the kernels from the cob. A giggle built up inside her like water ready to burst a dam, making her two long braids shake and her belly hurt. Then it erupted in a small burst of laughter. The laughter was contagious. Samuel did not know what was so funny but laughed along as best he could. "Thank you for showing us how to prepare the corn," he smiled. "It is quite delicious once you know how to prepare it."

Polly's face turned a touch of color for just a heartbeat. "You are welcome for the corn. It is good to share among friends." At that moment Bill came and sat next to Samuel. Samuel looked for the scowl that wasn't there.

"Speaking of sharing," Samuel said, scratching his chin. "Let us share with our new friends. We recently came into a bit of good tobacco."

Bill snickered then budded in, "Well, we received more a donation as it were."

Samuel gave Bill a wink then turned to Polly. "Maybe a few of your friends would like to share with us. Would you be so kind to ask them if they would like to smoke with us?"

Polly regarded Samuel for a moment in thought. She raised an eyebrow again as she deciphered his words. Samuel did not know if she understood.

He was just about to repeat himself when Polly spoke assuredly, "I will go see." Polly stood up, dusted herself off from the ground, and departed.

Polly returned with four men. The men approached the campfires cautiously as if they weren't sure they were welcome. The warriors from her tribe were dressed in breechcloths with leather leggings and beaded, cotton shirts. The Oneida men's heads were shaved except for a scalplock or a crest down the center of their head—the style known as a roach or a "Mohawk." One warrior wore a headdress that had two eagle feathers standing straight and one trailing behind. One man separated from the group and held out his hand to Samuel. His English was near perfect. "Greetings. My name is Jacob. This is Daniel, one of chief Shenendoah's sons. Han has a feathered headdress on his head and the tall one is John. Polly mentioned you would like to share some tobacco with us. We would be honored to share with our new friends."

Samuel shook Jacob's hand. "The honor is ours. We thank you for the food and your aid as scouts for the army. It has been a long time since we've had some good tobacco in camp. Anything decent we used up months ago. I look forward to sharing a donation made to us."

Polly's face abruptly turned to stone and gave a few sharp words in Oneida to the warriors, then departed to continue on her mission to teach the camp how to prepare the corn. Samuel made a mental note in his mind to ask about her look later. Pipes were passed around, as many as they could find within the cabins. A selection of wooden pipes in cherry, walnut, and maple appeared. The Oneida warriors brought out carved stone pipes that they brought with them. Samuel, Bill, and a half dozen Continentals formed a ring with the Oneida warriors around a large fire pit. Tobacco was passed out until the supply was empty. There was enough for every man to fill his pipe once. The men relaxed and began to smoke. Samuel took a deep inhale and exhaled the smoke into the air, watching it disappear in a cloud of smoke above them. "Tell me, Jacob. I couldn't help but notice Polly spoke something harshly to you before she departed. If I may ask without offense, what did she say?"

Jacob chuckled, "No offense taken. She wanted to remind us to represent the tribe with honor and not to get into any trouble. Not sure what trouble we could get into here." He peered into the charred bowl of his pipe. "We will be making some trouble as scouts against the British."

A tall Oneida warrior, introduced before as John, spoke slowly in rough but understandable English. "I wish we were able to bring more warriors, but we will make our numbers count."

Samuel nodded, exhaling a quick puff from his pipe. "We are honored to have you with us. I'm sure you will make your nation proud."

John continued: "You fight against the British for your independence. I ask, what kind of peace will the colonies form after the war. Will it look similar to the Haudenosaunee Confederacy after the war is done?"

Samuel looked puzzled. "What do you mean 'what kind of peace'?"

Hans, a muscled warrior, stood up slowly, not bothering to brush off the snippets of dirt that clung to him. He said, "How will our nations co-exist after this?"

Han's question sparked memories of Jacob's dream. Jacob spoke. "Samuel is a warrior like ourselves. It is not his decision. Do not burden him with this question. He fights where his leaders direct him."

Samuel scratched his head briefly in thought. "I would hope after this war is over that the colonies stay united in the cause of Liberty and I hope we will always live in friendship and peace with our Native American allies. Any men that bleed together in the common cause should be brothers to the end."

"Hear, hear," cried Bill, who was listening in on the conversation. Jacob puffed his pipe. He looked up at the sky then blew out a puffy grey cloud of smoke. "I hope that is so." He looked down from the sky. "I had a dream. Oh, forget about that. My nation has sacrificed much to help the colonists. I only pray our efforts and sacrifice shall not be forgotten. The future is what the future is. All bonds can break over time, when history is forgotten, except the bond with the Almighty. Should he will it, there shall be peace among our peoples. If he does not, there will be none. I am sure there is a clear resolve although it is hidden from us, yet the birth of that resolution shall be discovered."

"I don't be taken to the future, but every man here will never break that bond," said Samuel.

As the sun went down, the fire became bright and vivid, as though someone had shown a spotlight on it. As the night grew longer, they added more wood to colors of oranges, reds, and faint yellows. Laughter was heard as the men joked and traded stories. Any tension they held was leached out as they puffed their pipes. Late into the night, they laid back until darkness was cut only by the guiding light of the moon and the light of the flickering flames.

CHAPTER 17

ON THE HUNT AGAIN

Samuel was in a hurry. He wiped the sweat off his brow. With a quick trip to each, he had just said his goodbyes to his friends in the Rhode Island militia and Joseph Marin. The Rhode Island militia and Joseph's continental regiment would not be part of the reconnaissance mission. Although they may not shed blood together, not for kings, nor glory, they were brothers of Liberty. Samuel has selected as one of the players in the competitive game that the Oneida Warriors put together and he did not want to be late. Samuel was excited to be picked as one of the starting players. He looked forward to playing the game as an escape from his routine drudgery.

As Samuel moved swiftly to the game field, outside the camp, he took in the sun's rays that bounced happily, warming his skin, and he took deep breaths to take in the fresh smells of spring flowers lingering in the air. Birds chirped their songs as they danced through the sky to build new nests. What a change from the miserable winter, he thought to himself. From the cold dark winter of death to a charming spring day to play a game. I'm blessed to be breathing.

I must breathe the air and enjoy life for the sacrifices of those that could not be here. Too many notches on my belt knife.

It was the 17th of May, 1778. Marquis de Lafayette was anxious. George Washington had entrusted with him a great responsibility, and he did not want to let his friend down. Preparing for an early withdrawal of the British from occupied Philadelphia, Washington was sending Lafayette out to Barren Hill between Valley Forge and Philadelphia to block British supplies from coming in and harassment of the surrounding countryside. Because of the size of the reconnaissance force, this could be the first major confrontation with the British this year. The victory was sorely needed, for the public's will for independence was waning. Most European Allies were waiting on the sidelines and not supporting the floundering revolution until military success. The economy was in shambles, and the civil war against the loyalists was bitterly fought. Many began to think maybe it was better under the yoke of the British, especially the populace that had not chosen sides in the revolution.

The Oneida Warriors would be leaving the next day ahead of the full force to scout with some additional Continental scouts. Daniel, the Oneida Chief's son, had put together a game in the afternoon, to celebrate the upcoming departure of the force. Lafayette approved of the game wholeheartedly; it would help ease the men's minds before they marched out and subsequently his own. It would also be a great way to build comradery and loosen up the men prior to departure.

Samuel arrived just in time to the game field. A large area, more than 150 feet long and 10 feet across, had been prepared. The grass had been cut down with a scythe and copious amounts of water had been poured on the earth then trampled to smooth mud. Daniel, with enthusiasm, was explaining the rules of the game to the players. Jacob was giving further translation when necessary. The game would be a much-modified version of Snow Snake. This traditional Haudenosaunee game was played during the winter after the men of the villages returned from their annual hunting trip. The fun, sometimes intense, matches were designed to show off each village's ability. It was often referred to as a medicine game; besides sport and comradery, it lifted the hearts of men enduring deep winters.

The snakes were made from flattened, carved pieces of wood, made to look like a snake. To make it easier to throw, one end of the snake was notched and the other end was bent up slightly. The objective of the game would be to throw the wooden snakes through the smooth mud troughs created on the field at the farthest distance possible. Teams would alternate tosses. The total distance that the snakes traveled would be added together and the longest total distance would be crowned the winner.

Everyone that wanted to toss the snakes would have their turn but the first two teams were handpicked for a fun competition. The Continentals chose six, matched with an even number of Oneida warriors. To make the game more competitive they gambled for stakes. The Oneida wagered new hides, furs, and beaded wampum belts. The Continentals would wager gingerbread donated by Philadelphia baker Christopher Ludwig and six new Continental coats paid for by Hamilton and Lafayette. A large crowd, a few hundred men, surrounded the field to watch the contest.

"I see ye arrived in time, won't miss a thing. I don't reckon much about the game but it should be some good sport," said Bill.

"Don't rightly know how I got picked to play. I don't know if I should feel blessed or cursed," said Samuel.

Bill grinned. "I regard it's blessed if you doth well. I dunno why they picked thy. A smart one tis is. Might be if Washington discusses matters with ye. Which side are thou supposed to pick if a betting man?"

"The right one," said Samuel.

"Be thinking we ain't got a fool's chance of winning if it's their game. If I was betting, I'd bet the whole arm on them."

"Oh yeah? Are you taking sides against us now?"

"In this. I be thinking so. Right as rain on that one. Shh! Lafayette gonna speak."

"As a beacon of friendship, we play this match. We are grateful for the support of our new allies. They hath sacrificed much to aid us. Friendship is aye pure and as a bundle of joy which only needs moe and moe nourishment to grow. Ne'r shun true friends or take 'em for granted. We may join various people at diverse phases of our life. Many may counterfeit to be our friends yet hie by outward sparkle." He drew out his saber and pointed it to the sky. "Well, the victor will hie the spoils. Hast upon't men and enjoy yourselves. We shall see the fog of battle anon."

The first player up was Daniel. The proud warrior hurled the snake-like spear. It bounced out of the muddy trough quickly but managed a good distance of sixty feet. Next to play was Samuel. He had no clue how to play. He figured to toss it underhand for more accuracy. With a grunt, he swung his arms and tossed the snake. The snake smacked the ground about ten feet then bounced a few feet more. The crowd burst out laughing. Samuel snorted, "It tis be harder than it looks."

Daniel wiped the smirk from his face. "'Tis hard for a beginner and made even more challenging by mud versus snow. I am the best player in my village because of the practice." He puffed out his chest.

"Best player? To me maybe," Jacob added.

"Well, you'll get thy chance Jacob, thy next," Daniel mumbled sarcastically. Jacob grabbed the wooden snake and hurled it with all his strength. Even with lions' strength, it would have been useless; it stuck in the mud, easily scoring more than Samuel but well short of Daniel.

"Re-do methinks because of the mud!" Jacob protested. Then he folded his arms in mock frustration.

"I don't regard so, a play is a play, do not be a sore loser," said Daniel. The play continued until it was Daniel's last time up. He wound up with all of his might and threw. The snake slipped out of his hand and actually went backward." The crowd roared with laughter.

"Best player in the village?" Jacob beamed. More laughter.

The game continued with the Oneida Warriors easily winning the match. The game was hardly an equal match. The Continentals were crushed despite Daniel's final pathetic game points. Graciously accepting defeat, the losers gave out their wager. Memories of this day would echo for a long time. Laughter abounded so welcomely in contrast to the hunger and miserable winter at Valley Forge. The Oneida Warriors would be moving out tomorrow in advance of the Continental Regiments the day after. The advance towards the British was beginning this year with hopes for victory.

CHAPTER 18

BATTLE OF BARREN HILL

O n May 18, Lafayette left Valley Forge with approximately two thousand soldiers under his command and a few artillery pieces. They would be turning south after crossing the Schuylkill River, to take up a position at Barren Hill. This reconnaissance force marched out early in the morning into the surrounding woods. Men marched crunching over patches of leaves and branches that took over the ground, keeping a watchful eye for any British scouts. By the late morning after traveling for some time, they were in a heavily wooded area. The strong scent of a damp forest filled the men's noses. The forest was a buzz of life. Birds could be heard chirping in the tall trees and chipmunks played on the forest floor.

Samuel was at the head of the column. He kept an eye on his men and the forest. In a moment of excitement, one of his men stepped on a rotten branch and a red and black garter snake slivered its way out from underneath startling the man. The surrounding soldiers all laughed as the serpent zoomed away. Samuel had to quiet the men before it turned into a ruckus. He even came close to using his tricorn hat to whack some men. Other than the snake fun the march was rather uneventful.

Prior to nightfall, the rebel force arrived at Barren Hill. Under the light of a full moon, Samuel's brigade with most of the force was ordered to set up camp on the high ground, near a church, facing south with the artillery. The remaining force was positioned a little distance away to guard the road that led west. The Oneida Warriors remained out scouting. You would have thought the British scouts escaped capture and discovered that the rebels were nearby and moved to seek their destruction, but an unknown traitorous rebel spy gave them the intel. Late in the evening under darkness, General James Grant and a large British force, outnumbering the rebels four-to-one, was sent toward Barren Hill. His plan was to encircle Lafayette's force trapping them like a vice, cutting off any avenue of retreat. The British waited for the first light to attack and wipe out the rebels.

In the morning fog grew thick to dampen the men's spirits. It was difficult for the men to see at any long distance. They strained their eyes at the movement of shadows. Grey clouds moved in to cover the sky. The birds chirping, the men became used to; it began to slow down then stop entirely. The British began their attack. Samuel was within Lafayette's left flank, where a body of elite assault troops, dragoons (unmounted cavalry), and grenadiers (specialized grenade and assault troops), moved forward towards them. Samuel was close enough to see the grenadiers wearing their bearskin caps making the soldiers appear tall and menacing; they halted just opposite Samuel's position. The Continentals formed a line hastily and prepared for the assault.

"Steady men. Bear the line! Remember thy training, and remember the atrocities they have delivered to our homeland," hollered Samuel.

Many in the Continental first ran and fell quickly as the dragoons opened accurate deadly fire. Samuel fired his musket with the remains of the first rank and worked to reload quickly. He grabbed a cartridge from his belt and tore it open with his mouth and then poured the powder down the barrel. He dropped a lead ball down the barrel and quickly rodded it. He set his musket to his shoulder. A loud crack of fire and a grenadier fell from the shot. Musket balls whisked back and forth. A Continental fell on the side of Samuel. Samuel reloaded as fast as he could. Somehow the rebel line still held under punishing continuous fire. The woods were filled with the smoke and the smell of discharged powder from the heavy firing. The stink of gunpowder was so much that Samuel had to exhale to clear his lungs. With a groan, the Continental to Samuel's other side fell.

Suddenly he heard a spluttered cry from the British line, "Fix Bayonets!" The British were attempting to finish their enemy now. Samuel cocked his musket and fired his last shot. The Continentals scrambled to fix bayonets as the British charged. The font ranks crumbled as the armies broke apart and slugged it out. It was absolute chaos. Man to man combat, bayonet versus bayonet. Horrible-sounding groans and screams of men being stuck like animals. It was war at its worst, both savage and bloody. Fortunately, Steuben trained his men well. The Americans fought back and with desperate cries from their officers were able to slowly form firing lines, small at first, then expanding to larger groups.

Samuel blocked with his musket what would have been a mortal blow from a grenadier, one aimed for his heart with a bayonet strike. With his block, he was moved off balance and fell back to the ground face forward. He spun to his back, removed his pistol, and shot the attacker point-blank in the chest. The man staggered but did not fall. Scrambling up, Samuel stabbed the attacker in the throat with the tip of his bayonet. Blood poured out from the grenadier as he uselessly clutched his throat to hold back the blood. In the time it took for a quick breath Samuel just barely dodged another bayonet from a savage attacker with eyes of pure hate. The attacker managed to hit Samuel with the butt of his weapon and Samuel collapsed to the ground, his musket dropping from his hands. The attacker reversed his weapon with his bayonet about to plunge into Samuel. A quick prayer was uttered as Samuel prepared to receive death's embrace.

A gaudy thud. The attacker took a round in the chest and he stumbled, his bearskin hat fell from his head, a few more bullets tore into him, finishing him off. A line had formed behind Samuel, controlled by a screaming officer. It was Lafayette himself. Samuel bent down close to the forest floor. He could feel the blood dripping from his head. Suddenly he felt a piercing pain, a bullet ripped and crushed through the tissue of his shoulder. Exploding pain nearly blinded Samuel but he had to do one thing. Get the heck out of there. He began to crawl on his hands and knees toward the Continental line of fire to seek cover. The enemy began to form a line to counter the rebels. Bullets whistled over his head as Samuel moved as quickly as he could, which was much like a tortoise. Blood and dirt prevented full vision. He crawled on, hoping to reach protection.

As Samuel drew closer to safety. A continental soldier broke ranks to drag him the rest of the way. Behind the line, Samuel struggled to his feet, then used his hat to wipe the gunk from his eyes. He wobbled sideways and barely caught himself from falling. Blood flowed down his sleeve from his shoulder wound, from a gash on his cheek and an open scalp. He watched as the Continental line moved forward with a banner that spelled the words "Don't tread on me." He drew strength from the passing banner and fought back pain to rejoin the attack. He forced himself up and searched around, looking for a musket to rejoin the ranks. It did not take him long to find one. It had a bayonet on it stuck into a red coat. He removed it, reloaded the weapon, and proceeded to move slowly back to the line. He took a position towards the rear. The line was much larger now but it appeared about to crumble. The British line was amassing a large amount of fire that was ripping through the field.

At this critical moment, the Oneida Warriors appeared out of nowhere with the American scouts. With a loud war cry, they attacked fiercely and savagely. They quickly leaped from horses to fight in close combat with tomahawks and spears. The American scouts provided up-close support with musket fire. The bold attack staggered the British and gave them pause. In desperation a British officer hollered, "charge!" then chaos ensued. An attacker's punch to his head left Samuel staggering but he took the pain. He slashed the attacker in the face with his bayonet. The man took off screaming. A movement caught him from his side and he turned to stab. It was Jacob—he recognized the Oneida warrior. Jacob's face was covered in war paint. "We reckoned you could use some help," Jacob shouted over the noise of battle. Samuel winced from the pain and shot Jacob an indignant look, but his eyes twinkled with sport.

"Welcome to the soiree," Samuel muttered gruffly. The men nodded to each other as a crack sounded and Jacob took a shot directly at his abdomen. With a cry of pain, Jacob slumped over. Samuel looked for the shooter but could not find him, he stood over the bleeding Jacob protecting him with his body. The shot should have been mortal but it did not penetrate deep. The musket ball struck the bottom of his Continental uniform that he had won at the snake game, striking a button. Jacob struggled to get up and he leaned on Samuel; his own trembling limbs would not support him completely. Both men, leaning against each other back to back, prepared to fight to the end.

The end for them did not come. Han approached the pair with tremendous speed. His face was cold as death and hard as stone. Blood was splattered all over him but no visible wounds were his. Han's eyes glistened with battle lust. With one look at Jacob, his muscled shoulders squared, he picked up Jacob and carried him. Samuel followed them limping behind and nearly passed out from his loss of blood.

The Continental drums called for retreat as the British numbers became too many to fight. The heroic actions of the Oneida Warriors with American scouts provided a needed distraction against the British while the army started their retreat back to Valley Forge. Their action's allowed Lafayette to make a speedy retreat with minimal losses. The Native American warriors were the last to cross the Schuylkill River. It is thought that six Oneida warriors were killed during the engagement, including a tribal Sachem, Thomas Sinavis. The bodies were taken to Peter's Church Cemetery in Barren Hill and buried. Washington publicly praised the bravery and timeliness of the Oneidas attack. If not for the Oneida and American scouts heroically engaging the British, Lafayette's force, nearly a fifth of the American army, would have been slaughtered and may have caused a different outcome for the war. Lafayette escaped with odds stacked heavily against him, and although he lost the battle, he gained respect from Washington.

CHAPTER 19

SQUARE ANOTHER DAY

Lafayette's forces marched back to Valley Forge along a small road concealing them from the British. The dirt road was low to the ground with plenty of forests to hide it from their sight. The wounded trudged slowly at the rear of the retreating column. Only a few were carried by litter; mostly they used makeshift crutches and volunteers bearing the weight of their comrades. One of the drummers for the regiment, a tall boy for his young age of thirteen, stood close by Samuel's side, fearful he would collapse. The boy was not helpful, especially because the boy would not keep quiet. "We gave as good as we got, I reckon. They'll think twice before they smack with us again. Glad we ain't too far from camp."

Samuel stubbed his foot on an exposed root. The pain made it all the way to his shoulder and he groaned. "Do you think maybe you could keep quiet for a while? I can't rest my shoulder; at least let me rest my thoughts for a while."

Lafayette walked among the wounded. Despite the defeat, he was lucky only a small number were killed or wounded thanks to the scout's skirmish that halted the British. The casualty number disturbed Lafayette, who felt the burden of his responsibility. Lafayette approached Samuel. Lafayette's expression softened. "I praise you for your service. Although the enemy took the field you men fought with great courage. If I were a poet I'd put my thoughts to quill. I encourage you to heal fast and help us hunt more redcoats." He laid a hand on Samuel's arm gently for a brief second then he moved on to the next wounded.

Carts and wagons met the wounded partway to camp and took them directly to hospitals surrounding Valley Forge. The last place on earth soldiers wanted to be. Hospitals were feared as a place of death for wounded soldiers. For some, a loss of a limb was a death sentence. It was common practice if a limb was badly putrid or fractured to amputate it. Only a third of amputees actually survived the surgery. There were no pain killers and most of the patients were given alcohol and a stick to bite down on while the surgeon worked. Two assistants would hold them down. A good surgeon could perform the entire process in under a minute, after which the patient usually went into shock and fainted. This allowed the surgeon to stitch up the wound, and prepare for the next amputation. Most amputees died of infection, a result of not properly cleaning instruments after surgeries.

Samuel woke and wished he did not. He remembered the doctor treating his shoulder before passing out from the pain. His head throbbed as he opened his eyes. He was laying on a straw cart. His head was bandaged tightly in a cloth, most likely scraps of an old shirt. The shoulder was wrapped in a similar dressing. Trying to move his right shoulder he gasped as flashes of pain and nausea stopped his attempt. He peeked around his surroundings. Men were recovering in various states with faces sagging with weariness and worry. Some with hands pressed in prayer.

"I see you awake, by the look on your face, maybe not happy to be so," a voice called from his neighbor in a cart beside him. Samuel recognized Jacob. Jacob sat up slowly. His shirt was off, exposing a bandage wrapped around his stomach area. The war paint on his face was streaked from sweat and grime. "I was lucky; only a nasty cut from the bullet that glanced off my belly, and some decent bruises. I watched 'em work on your shoulder. They probed for a musket ball or fragment yet could not find any. I pray 'were a clean shot and the bullet went through and a special prayer that you never take the fever. A doctor was going to pour mercury on your wound to prevent festering but was stopped by a woman with her hair high in a knot and with the look of an eagle in her eyes. She was afraid the mercury would harm you."

"Sounds like Molly, as tough as nails is she. Me and my friend Joseph met her when we delivered patients here." He frowned. "Never thought I'd be lying here." He looked hard at Jacob. "I've seen so many friends get wounded or die. I've escaped through luck alone. I remember my friends who passed with a small notch on my knife handle."

"To honor 'em with a corporal notch on thy knife handle. You honor 'em more I think by truly bearing their remembrance in thy heart. Did you escape through luck? You never value yourself that much if thou regard that. You are engaged in a losing broil dissatisfied with imperfections in life. Life hath imperfections in all areas of everyone's existence; if thou eliminate that belief of luck you'll begin to discover the perfection in life itself."

Samuel struggled to sit up trying not to move his wounded shoulder. The slightest movement only brought agony. He noticed Polly Cooper move in front of Jacobs' cart. She lowered her head slightly and fixed her eyes on Jacob. Jacob mirrored, staring back. Polly placed her fists on the side of her skirt. She spoke in the native tongue, "Jacob, I told you to be careful of the bullets."

Jacob gave a grin than an exasperated sigh. "Maybe I just wanted to see your lovely face again."

Polly's voice faltered, "You men fought bravely, I'll give you that. You saved the day and allowed the colonists' army to withdraw in proper retreat." Samuel did not know what they were discussing but guessed it would be fun to watch, so he tried to adjust himself to watch the show. He grimaced in pain. Polly noticed Samuel's attempt to get comfortable. She reached over to help him and frowned when she looked at the dressing on his shoulder. Blood was beginning to dampen through. Polly went over to Jacob and she carefully undressed his wound looking it over thoughtfully then re-wrapped it. Then she looked at Samuel. In English, she spoke," May I?" Samuel nodded approval. He took a deep breath as Polly gently undid his bandage. She then spoke to Jacob in her native tongue.

Jacob translated: "Polly doesn't trust the doctors here. She brought a honey dressing for me but after looking over my injury she feels you need it more. It should help prevent infection."

Samuel did not hesitate. "I am honored. Please let her know I would be grateful if she applies it." Polly applied the honey dressing mixed with herbs, using tender hands; the application did not hurt. After the wound was re-wrapped, Polly looked into Samuel's eyes and affectionately gripped his good shoulder then gave Jacob clear instructions on what she wanted Samuel to know about his wound care. Samuel's exhausted body had gone through a lot of trauma. He listened to Polly converse with Jacob unable to comprehend what they were saying to each other. Exhaustion swept over Samuel and his eyes became heavy and he drifted off into a deep sleep. He never saw Polly leave.

Just after first light, Samuel felt groggy. He looked to his side at the cart next to him to see Jacob was gone and a new arrival had taken his place. A heavily wounded man with a recovering leg amputation. Samuel said a short prayer in his head that the man would survive. The pain in his shoulder still ached and throbbed, however, it was reduced. A doctor came by to take a look at his shoulder and scoffed at the honey dressing, but he told Samuel that no further harm would come from the dressing and if it gave the patient more hope the better. But Samuel had faith in the dressing, faith that the Native

American generations that embraced nature would have more of a clue of its mysteries than the colonists ever dreamed.

Samuel's stay in the hospital was filled with boredom. His only entertainment was eating and visits from Polly and his friends. The food was great, for those that could eat. Christopher Ludwick, the German-born gingerbread baker, appeared daily and personally passed out delights for the men, including warm pretzels. Polly without fail came each day to change his honey dressing. He tried to make conversation with her frequently, but she said only a few words. Always quick to be done with her task so she could return to her work at Valley Forge.

The pain and discomfort in his shoulder improved. He even was able to get off his cart and walk around. From the hardwood floor to the paneled walls it was depressing to be in the hospital. Many dispirited and grim faces watched him pass, people who knew they were trapped and if they made it out they would never be the same. Besides, physically injured the soldier would feel mentally rootless, unable to continue fighting alongside his brothers.

CHAPTER 20
VICTORY IN DEFEAT

Bill and Joseph were very glad to hear that gangrene or fever were not setting in. Bill was disturbed in his voice. "It was an embarrassment at Barren Hill. The Pennsylvania militia guarding the west flank scattered at the sight of the British troops. That dank militia offered no resistance and failed to notify Lafayette of the attack."

Samuel felt well enough to razz Bill. "Outnumbered with a wave of swarming red of dragoons and grenadiers, they fled like sheep with a lion charging at them. There is no crime against foolishness and dead men can't be bore accountable for their actions. How wouldst you fare with a lion charging you?"

Bill's thoughts floated through his head about to erupt. "I guess a herd of sheep canst fight lions. Yet we were not all sheep. The Continentals stood their ground and went toe to toe with 'em. Takes a lion to fight a lion."

Joseph cleared his throat. "We brought you some effects from your knapsack. He poured out the contents on the cart. "Your shaver, dental powder, and stuff." Joseph winked. "Some rum to share. Oh, you won't be needing that, I'll keep it safe for you." Joseph held out Samuel's knife.

"No, I'll keep it," said Samuel.

Joseph gave him Samuel a quizzical look. "Alright, whatever."

"Hey, guys," Bill said. "Why don't sheep remember things thou say to 'em? Because all goes in one ear and out the udder." Although the joke was not funny they laughed, and only a stone fellow could do anything but join in the mirth.

"Get better soon, Samuel, there's a word we will be on the march again soon," spoke Joseph said. Our forces may be scrambled of colonial eggs yet we are not beaten. We're going to win this war. Especially men like you. Durable as iron."

Bill and Joseph visited as long as they could until they were kicked out of the hospital for singing bawdy revolutionary songs too loud. They had decided to help with the bottle of rum Samuel did not remember keeping.

On his last day before release, Molly, aka Molly Pitcher, visited Samuel. She gave Samuel a thorough look over his wounds. "I'm glad you are doing better. You may leave tomorrow morning but hear me, no weight on that shoulder for some time. She arched her eyebrow. "If you re-injure it we may not treat it again," she said with a grin.

Samuel winked. "I warrant to take care of it. Let it rest some, I shall need to improve to dispatch more red coats with it."

I'm sure thou shall, 'tis said thou fought bravely at Barren Hill. Now again, do not be stupid with thy injury. Then again I do be talking to a man." Molly shook her head and moved on to another patient.

Samuel went to bed content that he would get out of the hospital tomorrow and re-join the army, but his anxiety caused by anticipation made it difficult to sleep. It took hours until he drifted off to restless sleep. In his dream, grey clouds moved in and thunder roared. The wind blew in fierce gusts. He was standing on a beach wearing simple farmers clothes he was used to wearing before the uncomfortable

Continental uniform became his everyday apparel. He eyed the water, observing a host of British warships. They were anchored in the act of sending out a large wave of transport ships loaded with royal marines. Under the cover of darkness, they landed, unloaded, and immediately spread out. After a short time, the unmistakable sound of sporadic musket fire met them. Undaunted, the marines continued to arrive. The militia could not possibly hold the red tide that was coming for them. British officers shouted, "Dress in ranks!" and they returned a steady hail of fire back at the militia. Infrequently the militia returned fire until their sounds vanished. They obviously fled in retreat; the British marines were stubborn foes once onshore.

Samuel next found himself wandering over the battlefield. The British had already cleared out their dead. The militia's bodies remained where they fell to be recovered later by whatever remained of the militia. He walked towards where the patriots attempted to defend their position using the thick brush for cover. A tattered flag with the words "Don't tread on me" lay on the ground. A few poor souls lay there never to breathe again. He gasped when he recognized the corpse of his younger brother. Duncan had a hole in the center of his forehead where he was shot. Brother, I can't possibly compose your memory in a notch in my knife handle, the thought resounded in his mind. Samuel remembered in life Duncan had a ready smile and knowing eyes. In death he was ghostly pale, his lips bluish. Duncan's head suddenly lifted up. His bloodshot eyes bulged out looking ready to pop. He struggled to speak. It came out in a gurgle, "With my brother dead who will take care of the farm, the cause is lost. The cause is los—"

Samuel cried out, "I'm here brother. I'm he--."

Samuel woke in darkness with the foul scent of the hospital to welcome him. A smell that would always remind him of a butcher shop. He stretched his arms above his head and yawned. He left his bed then walked a short distance in the near darkness behind a small tree. He kicked the soft dirt with his heel making a large gash on the earth. He took out his knife and looked at the many notches cut into it. He placed the blade gently into the hole then swept dirt over it. He gave it a stomp for good measure.

Samuel returned to his cart and tried to let the thought of his brother go. It was only a dream, he told himself. He stayed awake to allow the visions of the night to give way to the day. In the morning he would be able to greet the sunlight on his own accord and get out of these dismal conditions. Most dreams fade with morning light but the vision from his dream clung as his last memory of the night that remained with him.

CHAPTER 21
THE OLD FOX

With the first rays of morning light, Samuel walked alone back to camp at Valley Forge. No longer confined to the hospital's cramped space, it was an abundant joy. The fresh air added to lift up Samuel's spirit. It gave a sensation there was no word for, it rendered the moment rich with vitality. Samuel was alive and he took nothing for granted. Thankful to have all his limbs intact. His family's farm would need him after the war ended. He gazed up at the sky and prayed a silent prayer in gratitude for his well-being.

Although the British won a victory at Barren Hill, they had observed a different American Army on the battlefield. Now the rebel army was ready to fight. Confidence, passion, and pride marked those who had survived the ordeal of Valley Forge. The Old Fox, General George Washington, had survived the winter at Valley Forge and had grown stronger. The British thought Philadelphia would be a difficult place to defend. Washington's command, which had once dwindled to a mere 5,000 troops, was now thought to be 13,000, perhaps larger than the British force in Philadelphia, and now that France was in the war, the city was also vulnerable to attack or blockade from the sea. The British decided to abandon the city and move forces back to their base in New York City. The British Army, including 3,000 loyalists, began the evacuation. The final evacuation of Philadelphia would be concluded on June 17. Washington planned to abandon Valley Forge and move across the Schuylkill River to set up camp a mile away. Washington determined to pursue the British and move to within striking distance.

Samuel arrived at camp and immediately checked in at his brigade command tent. Although not expected there was no welcome back ceremony. The tent was a buzz of activity. Preparations were underway for the army to depart and quickly move against the British retreating from Philadelphia. There was a great deal of work to be done before departure that included Washington's orders for work parties to clean up the camp filth. He instructed work parties to clean up the campground, bury all garbage and fill the latrines. Samuel was ordered to return to his men after a quick trip to supply to collect anything he needed. At supply, he swapped out his tattered, bloodstained waistcoat and jacket for a new one. He was offered a new musket but he declined. His musket, as well as his pistol, were kept safe with his men. His weapons were old friends he would no sooner depart.

He arrived at his cabin and found it empty with the exception of Bill sitting on the floor sharpening his bayonet. Bill looked upon Samuel with astonishment. He dropped the bayonet with a muffled curse and sat sucking on a nicked finger, staring at Samuel. "Welcome back," he said, rising and embracing Samuel. "I knew those lobster backs couldn't take you out of the fight. You just missed Jacob and that tall fella john. They were hither checking if you arrived yet from the hospital and they wanted to personally invite you to hast a meal with 'em this e' en at their quarters. They're preparing a meal for those they shed blood with at Barren Hill. I hear say, they are leaving soon and it's their way of saying goodbye."

Samuel frowned. "Leaving? They are some of the bravest warriors I have ever seen. You should have seen Han at the battle. It still gives me chills. A few thousand like him and the British will surely run from us at every battle."

"I believe you. Hey, I need to report to fill in some latrines and since you're probably not assigned to anything yet we could use all the hands we can get. If you're up for it?"

Samuel scratched his head. "I promised Polly not to do anything that would prevent my shoulder from healing. I've done enough exertion today with the walk and all. I'm going to rest for a while, maybe even nap. Make sure you wake me when you get back. We can visit the Oneida Warriors together this evening."

Bill smiled. "You got it, Samuel, you've earned some rest. Receiveth all you get now, we shall be fighting soon, got plenty of redcoats to send packing. Well, I must go now. My duty calls. Don't crave others to regard I'm a slacker."

* * *

Without the Revolutionary War, the Oneida Warriors would probably be with their families, getting ready for the day's chores around the farm, milking cows, and cutting firewood instead of wondering where the next fight would be. Daniel hurled the tomahawk straight at the wooden practice target, missing the center painted red. The sun was at full blast, and his shirt was off. Sweat glistened on his body and salty droplets flowed down Daniel's face. "So we are really going to leave?"

Jacob turned to face him. "Yes, Daniel, your father, and the clan mothers agree. Our homes are in danger!" Daniel moved to the target, removed his tomahawk then stepped back about twenty feet from the target.

"I understand, just not thrilled with the decision. We agreed to help them."

Jacob patted Daniel on the shoulder. "I'm sure it was not an easy decision to call us back. Here, let me have a go at that." Daniel handed the single-handed axe to Jacob. Jacob rocked the tomahawk back and forth with his wrist, feeling the weight, then launched the axe towards the target, hitting dead center.

Daniel chuckled. "You were always a better throw than me, not so much with Lacrosse." Jacob feigned a frown. Daniel laughed. When Daniel laughed, you could hear his joyful laughter from about a mile away. Daniel removed the tomahawk from the target and threw, missing the center again.

John and Han walked towards the pair. Han wiped his forehead with his hand. "We just spoke with mohawk, brother Atyataronghta or Colonel Louis Cook as he is named in English. He shall discuss with our warriors who remain about joining the 'Indian Rangers' of the 1st New York regiment, which already includes Tuscarora and Caughnawaga warriors. I fought with him at the Battle of Oriskany. Louis is a proven warrior and is fiercely loyal to the colonists' cause." John stepped forward and took the tomahawk from Daniel, inspecting it.

"The colonist's cause?" Daniel murmured. "Didn't they stir the pot? Didn't they dress like Mohawks and dump tea into that harbor?"

John rubbed the axe handle on his head gently. There was an edge to his eyes, which had seen too much blood. "Like us, their first cause is to protect homes and families. The British are dogs. Imagine the insult of quartering them in your home while your loved ones die to protect you against them. Do not judge your neighbor until you walk two moons in his moccasins." John hurled the tomahawk, striking the target dead center.

Daniel retrieved the tomahawk and motioned for Han to take it. "Ok, Han, it's your turn." Han waved Daniel off. Han took his own tomahawk from his belt, and with a quick motion hit the target dead center. Daniel glanced at the target, his face cast as deadpan as he could manage, yet he failed. There at the corner of his mouth began a smile. "Looks like more practice for me."

* * *

Samuel woke groggily as Bill shook him. The cabin was darker with the setting sun. "Wake up. Just got back from duty. We don't crave to miss it. I hark a feast is set by Oneida. I'm salivating!"

"I'm up. I'm up. I'm quite hungry also." Samuel ignored the pain in his shoulder, lifting himself out of bed. He splashed a cup of water on his face and combed his fingers through his hair. Perspiration still clung to Samuel's dirty cotton shirt. June's heat was coming with a vengeance, getting even with winter.

"Nobody cares what ye look like. Allow us to get going."

As they walked to the gathering they began to smell roasted meat. Their stomachs growled. A beautiful feast was waiting outside cabins that the Native American's lived in. A few wooden tables with pewter plates they borrowed from Lafayette were set up. They smiled as they looked at the wooden tables filled with wonderful food that seemed to sparkle from the light of tallow candles. Platters of fish perfectly cooked and vegetables rested around the table. A large wooden barrel promised a generous amount of rum. Their stomachs rumbled as they watched a juicy deer slowly roasting above a fire. Nobody dared touch the food or drink till opening prayer. The small crowd of Continental soldiers and Native Americans dispersed in conversation and waited.

Jacob spoke before the throng. "Before eating it is always good to take time and be thankful for food. I will keep prayer short for the sake of the hungry stomachs here. Lord, we are thankful for all you provide for us. We thank you for your mercy and your grace upon us. Let our brothers who have passed find their way to you. Amen."

The feast began. The hungry men attacked the tables piling food high on their plates. Samuel filled his plate then sat down on a soft, grassy patch devouring his meal. Bill found a spot next to him carrying an overflowing plate with a hunk of deer meat balancing on top.

Jacob approached. "Good to see you on your feet, Samuel," he said. "Your strength shows not only in your ability to persist but your ability to lead. Alas, I need to bid you farewell. I shall be leaving tomorrow with most of us to defend our home from other tribes and the British."

Polly pushed her way through a few people to look upon Samuel. Her face looked quizzical then she spoke to Jabob, who translated for her: "She wants to make sure you're letting your shoulder heal. You best mind her, she knows what is good for you. If you disappoint her I fear I could not protect you." Polly gave Jacob a look of daggers. She must have interpreted some of the English. Polly stormed off.

"Take care of yourself." Samuel cleared his throat. "It stinks to hear that you are leaving. Your warriors are handy i' a pinch. You surely saved the day for us at Barren Hill."

After the meal, the now stuffed men crowded in a cabin. Although the largest in camp, and with all the furnishings removed till only the floor remained, the size was not enough and the men spilled outside the door. The smoke from all the pipes passed around hit men hard in the cramped space. The sounds of coughing echoed.

Colonel Louis Cook entered the cabin. His head was shaved, with only a long patch of dark hair remaining in the center. He was dressed in a white hunting shirt with fringes, tied around the middle with a broad belt, in which was fastened a tomahawk, the shot bag, and a carved powder horn. He wore the pants of a Continental soldier. "Although the broil was lost at Barren Hill, we hast learned we are stronger together i' cause for Liberty. I would like to address the Native American warriors hither. The weakness of our foe makes us stronger. Should thee crave to see what your body shall look like tomorrow, look at thy thoughts today. A true warrior regards it as an honor to be selected for a difficult or dangerous office. We are as a string of beads united for a common cause to dispel the British. For those that remain here to fight with us, we welcome you to join the rangers of the first New York regiment. My friends, the leader of the Continental power, General George Washington, admires us for the ability to scout and fight. He and I ask you to join us in common cause protecting issues and homes. Great songs shall be sung in honor of this special regiment one day. Allow us to bleed as one with the Continentals and confound our foe." A few hoots and shouts of "Hear, hear!" came from the gathering. "If you have any interest, prithee find me."

The pipe smoke eventually became too much in the crowded cabin so the gathering moved outside. There were no complaints. The men continued to devour food and drink till the tables were empty. The feast now turned into a going-away party that went on into the night. Pipers, drummers, and fiddle were produced and everyone danced like they'd forgotten how to. The Native Americans later in the evening took out drums to beat on by hand, encouraging everyone to dance the traditional dances of the Earth Songs. Each song varies in speed and skill with dancers moving in a counterclockwise direction. An announcer introduced each dance in English. His job was to serve as a "caller," similar to the leader found in square dancing, providing instructions to the dancers as they move along to ensure everyone stays on a beat and is doing the correct steps. Laughter abounded. The Native Americans had a grand time laughing at the Continentals attempts to do the steps. The Continentals took it in good stride and laughed themselves.

As the night grew late, moonlight shone down, a diffuse glow, lighting the camp from pitch black to charcoal grey. The celebration would go on till early dawn. They celebrated not as Native Americans and Continentals but as brothers in arms. Everyone is equal when the musket balls are flying.

CHAPTER 22

FAREWELL MY BROTHERS

A strong breeze moved over the surrounding foliage, now deep green from embracing the sun. It was late morning in the middle of June. Samuel and a small crowd of continentals and militia gathered to watch the Oneida depart. The Oneida greeted them warmly.

"So 'tis adieu?" Samuel shook Jacob's hand. "We appreciate the help with our cause."

Jacob shook his head. "Sorry we leave so few. I wish it were not the case. You do now hast Polly. She is worth more than countless warriors. She is destined to be remembered in our history."

"We understand why so many of you must leave. I receive what thou say about Polly. She hath a firm-set sense of not giving up and doing what is right. Good luck on your trip home. May your return journey home be safe," said Samuel.

Jacob nodded. "Thank you. Days will pass and turn into years but I will always remember we fought together. We bled together. From this day forward I will call you brother. A brother sticks together through good times and ill."

"I like the sound of that. It does me good to gain more."

Jacob's voice took on a serious tone. "I grant thou this thought to keep ere I depart. You hast lost many friends in this horrible war. If aye you find yourself mourning, remember that grief is like a heavy set stone that can't be lifted alone. Share the burden of your thoughts with others."

In a staggered column the Oneida moved out towards their home. The Continentals watched as they disappeared out of sight. Although the Oneida warriors did not want to leave, their quick return home was necessary. The British with their Native American allies imminently threatened their families and homes. Thirty-four of the original fifty Oneida sent to help the colonists would return. Polly Cooper remained to help the Continental Army and the remaining Oneida joined Colonel Louis with other Native American allies in the Ranger Brigade.

Samuel paused for a moment looking back at camp. He watched as dark grey smoke drifted up from campfires into the sky. His mind reflected how nice to float away and go back home, at least for a little while. It would be far less dangerous working on his family farm than his current occupation. The assembly hustled back to camp. The army would be on the move soon. It would be Samuel's last trip to his cabin and a last chance to grab his few belongings. He took a deep breath and beheld his home for the past few months. He would not miss the smells of the cabin or the cramped space but he was grateful for the shelter it provided. With the warmth of summer, you would think it easy to forget the tough time spent during winter here, yet he would never forget that eternal winter at Valley Forge.

The door was wide open, still, he heard a rapping at it. A young, thin Continental soldier he did not recognize entered. "Begging your pardon, sergeant. I have a letter addressed to you if your name be Samuel Fox."

"I am he."

The young man gave a nod and handed the letter to Samuel.

"The letter was given to me by mistake," the young man said, shifting uncomfortably. "I have not opened it. You see my name is Samuel Knox. The post delivered it to me by mistake just before your deployment with Lafayette. You see the Letter F is smudged a good deal. I attempted a few times to deliver this to you when your brigade returned but you were away recovering at the hospital. I kept it safe for you."

"So you have, I thank you for your charge."

The young man relaxed. A slight cough. "Good day to you, sergeant."

Sergeant Samuel returned the greeting with a wink. "Good day to you, Samuel."

The young man departed.

Right away Bill entered, excitement in his eyes. "Ye best finish your goodbyes to this place, sergeant, they're about to order us to assemble." Samuel tucked the letter into his haversack and followed Bill to the assembly field outside camp. Drums sounded as the army began to muster. In no time loud shouts from the officers could be heard directing the brigades into position. Thousands of Continentals and Militia overflowed the assembly area. A light rain began to fall. Under a steady drizzle the army formed columns.

General Washington was noticed at a distance on a horse, surrounded by his aides, watching the assembly. When the column was completed, he rode slowly along the side of the column. He stopped at short distances greeting the men and making short conversation. Samuel was fortunate enough to be positioned outside the column. Washington stopped at Samuel and leaned forward. The general's eyes looked tired. "You seem to be steady on your feet. I'm sure Blue Skin will appreciate that." Washington motioned to his grey horse.

Samuel remembered smacking into the horse during that march to Valley Forge and felt a stinging embarrassment. He lowered his head a little bit. "My eyes can actually see what is in front of me this time, General. I'm sure Blue Skin will not be troubled today."

Washington chuckled. "The weather is definitely more a blessing today than 'twere on the march to Valley Forge. Now I know why birds fly south for the winter." Washington's warm smile slowly turned into a frown and his shoulders slumped. "I wish you boys did not suffer so much." Washington paused as a full minute passed in awkward silence.

Samuel pondered what to say. "General, the cause is worth any suffering. We fight for liberty even at the cost of our lives. It's not just empty words, 'Give me liberty or give me death.' This phrase will forever echo for those that value freedom."

Washington looked for a way to change the mood of the conversation to a more positive one. "Samuel, no longer shall I need your eye at Valley Forge, yet I would be grateful if thou continued to meet with me. 'tis valuable collecting thy thoughts to hark from non-officers."

"It shall be an honor to continue reporting to you, General. Should'st you ask me today, I'd report the men are excited to be moving and they feel ready to tackle the British. Content to send 'em packing."

"And that is what I intend to do. Winter and the time for idleness is past. We march now to take the fight to the British and bring the sons of liberty to victory," Washington said. In a brief flicker whatever weariness displayed in his eyes vanished as he drew his saber and held it high. He shouted, "Liberty or death!" to the cheers and hoots, then with a thud of his heel made his horse gallop away. He rallied the men with his aides desperately trying to keep up. Samuel hollered till his voice became hoarse, adding to the shouts erupting, as he held up his hat in one hand and his musket in the other.

In a long column, the Continental army began to march, a neatly advancing four-line column now that Steuben had taught them the deployment advantages of a multiline column compared to a single file one. The army would not march long. Washington was waiting for the British to make their move and would halt the army east a little over a mile from Valley Forge. The army sang as they marched.

Let Tyrants shak their iron rod,
And slav'ry clank her galling chains,
We fear them not,
We trust in God,
Our God Forever reigns.
Howe and Burgoyne and Clinton too,
With Prescot and Cornwallis join'd,
Together plot our Overthrow,
In one Infernal league combin'd.

When God inspir'd us for the fight,
Their ranks were broke, their lines were forc'd,
Their ships were Shatter'd in our sight,
Or swiftly driven from our Coast.

The Foe comes on with haughty Stride;
Our troops advance with martial noise,
Their Vet'rans flee before our Youth,
And Gen'rals yield to beardless Boys.

Song inspired by "Chester" a patriotic anthem composed by
William Billings

The rain stopped. Rapidly thinning gray clouds let through startlingly bright sunshine with vivid blue air. A beautiful, double rainbow formed, stretching across the sky. Its colorful hues kissed the earth. There would be no pot of gold at the end of it, but a motivated army protecting their homeland was better than one.

CHAPTER 23

DELAYED POST

The column arrived at their designated location in the late afternoon. Samuel quickly gathered the men in his charge. Including himself, the men totaled twelve. Their uniforms were clean and bright. Beyond the fresh uniforms, they held a new sense of worth like a transition from boys to men learned literally by blood, sweat, and tears. "Alright, lads, I know you have plenty of shot and powder but before we go setting up tents I want to see what else you brought. Dump 'em!" Samuel inspected the piles and snatched a pair of socks. He's a dorbel. How many times do I have to go over this? "Joshua, you have only one pair of stockings here. Finally, we actually hast a supply. You were told to grab at least two pairs. Why didn't you grab an extra pair?" Joshua gave a dumbstruck look. He was not the brightest candle even on a good day, but he never slacked from labor. "Doth you see the value in an extra pair?" Joshua nodded. "Then get going."

"Ahem," coughed Bill.

"Yes," said Samuel.

"Been thinking, don't know if enough shot was issued for all the redcoats to be killed."

"Then I suppose we will have to find more on the battlefield," said Samuel.

A crowd of voices: "Hear, hear!"

Samuel rolled his eyes. "Alright, hie set up those tents and be glad you have all your supplies else you are expecting extra duty like Joshua will be receiving. Move out."

The camp was a mismatch of tents. Tents varied from linen to hempen threads. They were imported to the colonies from a number of countries, including Russia, Germany, Finland, and Sweden. Samuel's men would take up two tents. They would be crowded, with five or six men sharing a wedge-shaped tent. The chances of not touching the sides were slim. After their tents were set up, they joined others setting up camp.

Samuel tried to avoid any forced movement with his injured shoulder but failed miserably. Waves of pain forced him to stop when his body had enough. Reluctantly, he watched the labor, annoyed he could not join in. It was dark when the camp setup was finally completed. Samuel went to his shared tent. He rolled his blanket on the ground, wincing with agony. His overworked shoulder was still unhappy with him. He took off his jacket and waistcoat and rolled them into a pillow. He untucked his cotton shirt that still clung to his skin from perspiration.

"So I hear ye are stuck with us, Washington's guard didn't want ye," said Bill.

"What?"

"Just kidding, thanks for staying. Ye been a good man in broil and a decent sergeant to boot."

"Thanks, someone needs to keep this motley crew in order. More than the guard needs me." Samuel winked.

Samuel pulled off his shoes, stockings, and stretched his toes out. He waited for the men to settle, stretched out on his blanket, then lit a candle to read his brother's letter while lying on his bed. The letter was 2 pages.

Dear Brother,

I hope this letter finds ye well. Again no word yet on Mother and Father thou I did not expect to hear anything. Newport is a prize the British will no sooner release. The British continue to cause mischief along the coast. Rhode Island has nearly 400 miles of coastline but we do the best we can to protect it.

I was thinking late about home and after we won this war. I do not wish to return to farming. I'm sure Father will not be happy. Elija Barton in my brigade has agreed to take me on as an apprentice chocolate maker. I'll be taught to roast cocoa beans and winnowing to separate out the nibs to grind and how to mix in sugar cane and molasses to make chocolate bars and drink. As you already know, since the tea tax many have switched to coffee and chocolate drinking.

I was also thinking of Mary Campbell. Always had a fancy for her. When I return I will ask her parents for permission to court her. I may be in a hard slog if Father does not agree. Any influence you could give on the matter would be welcome. I know Father has a different plan for my future but I chose to go my own path.

I will tell you more in person when I see you next. May the good Lord protect you till we meet again.

Duncan Fox

Page 2 of the letter.

Samuel,

It is with deepest regrets that I must tell you that your brother Duncan has passed away. We found this letter in Duncan's possessions. The cursed bloody flux took him (Dysentery). The drudgeries of his illness continued until they were released to God by sweet death. His brothers at arms have combined efforts for his proper burial.

Elijah Barton

Samuel's brain stuttered inside his skull. Thoughts led him to a flash of anger and he crumpled up the letter in his fist. Lost in the moment he punched his makeshift pillow, then rested his head in his hands. Eyes welled up and he wept.

CHAPTER 24

SORTING OUT THE MIND

A dream can be sweet, clear, and refreshing. It can also be bitter, strange, and crushing. Dreams are where you play out your deepest fits of hunger and fears, vivid and powerful; at times you don't realize you're in one. Samuel's dream took him back home to his family's farm in Newport, Rhode Island. There were no shaggy dogs to greet him when he arrived, nor the aroma of his mother's cooking in the kitchen. A feeling grew in him that something was not right. The feeling not only persisted but also grew stronger. He opened the worn door to the farmhouse and called out, "Mother, Father, I'm home!" Only silence answered. His hair stood up. He dashed through the house searching for them but he found not a soul. If Father is not here he must be in the field. He ran off to the field to see if his father was there. Nothing at the green wheat field, only a scythe resting on top of a pile of bent-over stalks. Cursing his luck, he ran back home and decided to wait till they returned. He sat outside the front door on a large millstone that was used as a step to the entrance. He anxiously waited, watching for his parents' return.

A vast blanket of white fog settled in. His heart pounded with excitement as he caught sight of a Landau carriage drawn by two horses, moving slowly up the dirt road to his home—well, barely a road, more a large path with plenty of crabgrass and weeds. The fog skirted around the carriage making the view of it more difficult. The carriage came closer with the sound of dirt and stone kicked up as it moved. It was painted black with decorative gold trim, doors with a gold raven on each. It was driven by well-dressed coachmen dressed all in black. The carriage came to a halt. Getting off his seat, the driver climbed down then opened the door for his passengers with a face that looked cut from stone. Mother and Father. They appeared pale as corpses with eyes slightly bulging, bags under their eyes. His Father's face looked cold as death. "There, there, Martha. It will be alright."

Mother wept and sputtered, "My boys, my boys. They're both gone."

What is she talking about? I'm right here. Samuel stood up; drawing a deep ragged breath, he shouted as loudly as he could, "Mother! Father! I'm here!" They did not hear his cry. Samuel jumped off the stone step and ran towards them. "Mother! Father! I'm here!" His parents were oblivious. Samuel reached for them and his hands passed through them. He let go a blood-curdling scream.

Samuel woke with a loud cry following his nightmare. He startled the men in his tent that had been fast asleep. Some jumped up thinking the camp was being attacked. The cramped tent stirred with movement with a few knocking into each other. "It's nothing! Back to bed, just a bad dream," Samuel's voice faltered. Samuel was glad his red face was hidden in the darkness of the tent.

Bill shouted, "Must have been some charming dream. Ye woke the whole friggin' tent and gave us a fright." He cast out a long yawn. "Get yourself to bed, boy's, morrow shall be hither soon, best to face it with a good night's sleep." The already tired men settled down quickly and fell back to sleep. Samuel could not even find a perturbed sleep; it deserted him entirely. He stayed awake, his dreadful thoughts twisting and turning.

At first light, Samuel dressed quickly and proceeded outside the tent still tucking in his shirt. The cramped tent was not the solitude nor sanctuary he needed to clear his mind. In a meandering walk around camp, he kicked loose stones. I am proud I joined and I have never given a thought to losing my life until now. Was it just youthful exuberance? 'm in the army. What did I think could happen to me? Never a thought to consider my parents if they lost both their sons. Am I so selfish? I did join first. If only my brother just stayed home? Maybe he would still be alive.

Samuel's parents intended to have many children, but it was not meant to be. They lost many children to illness and disease, most before the age of two. That war was not only fought by orphans and childless men, he understood, but it did not soothe him. He had witnessed so much death from battle and disease, so many friends cast to memory, and now his brother. He reasoned to toss his fate to whatever path lay before him, whatever the Almighty made clear. Still, his thoughts were troubled and he fought to ease them. It was necessary to keep his mind sharp for the battlefield for his life as well as the lives in his charge. The words of Jacob echoed, Aye you find yourself mourning, remember grief is a heavy set stone that can't be lifted alone. Share the burden with others.

Dragging his steps, Samuel returned to his men. They were sitting on a patch of crushed grass just outside their tents making a breakfast of milk combined with bread. They were laughing and roughhousing around the campfire. Bill stood up when Samuel arrived. "Cato Bannister of the Rhode Islanders was looking for ye. I told him ye would be back soon. Here, go fetch your cup. I brewed some tea for ye, as good as a King is served. From the look of glazed eyes, ye can use it."

Samuel returned with his tin cup, plate, and spoon. Bill poured the tea and tossed Samuel a chunk of bread. Samuel began ripping the bread into small pieces on his plate, then poured a little fresh milk on top of the bread from a redware pitcher. He tasted the tea. His nose wrinkled and lips moved but he fought back the urge to spit out the over-brewed tea. Sipping the tea, he forced it down, putting on a good face and he made sure to give Bill a look of appreciation.

Samuel was just slurping up the rest of his mushy bread as the division commander appeared, General Peter Muhlenberg. Muhlenberg was a square fellow with heavy eyebrows that always seemed drawn in thought. He was known to have cast off his minister robes for command at the onset of the Revolution to the chagrin of his family. His brother Fredrick, who was also a minister, did not approve of him going into the army until the British burned down his own church in front of him. "Good morning, lads, do you have time for prayer with me. Would do your souls good to give your supplications to the Almighty." Muhlenberg brought out his Bible from his coat and read, "To everything, there is a season, and a time to every purpose under the heaven: A time to be born, and a time to die; a time to plant, and a time to pluck up that which is planted; A time to kill, and a time to heal; a time to break down, and a time to build up; A time to weep, and a time to laugh; a time to mourn, and a time to dance; A time to cast away stones, and a time to gather stones together; a time to embrace, and a time to refrain from embracing; A time to get, and a time to lose; a time to keep, and a time to cast away; A time to rend, and a time to sew; a time to keep silence, and a time to speak." He paused. "A time to love, and a time to hate; a time of war, and a time of peace." He finished reading and said, "And this is the time of war. The good shepherd will fight off the wolves. Bow your heads." Peter finished with the Lord's Prayer, then they prayed with the men for the souls of their departed brothers to rest in peace in God's loving embrace.

Samuel pulled Peter aside after service. "I had a horrible dream last night. To compose a long story short it got me thinking. My parents have only me now. My brother has just died. I am so deeply troubled by it. I hast to get the image of mourning parents out of mine head. Do you have any words of hope to help ease my tortured mind?"

"I am sorry to hear about thy brother. Everyone dies, my friend. Life on this earth is short. Only a blink of an eye. What we doth i' this life doth not echo an eternity. The next life is where eternity lives in heaven. Should thee die thy parents shall find a way to move on. Trust in God, put thy heart at ease." Peter sighed softly. "It is easier quoth than done, believe me, but take steps even if it's a crawl. At first, these steps shall lead thou towards the right path and still waters of thy swinish mind. If you shall ever feel death's embrace, you shall be at peace in your heavenly eternity."

Samuel took a deep breath. "Th--."

Bill bumped into Samuel. "Sorry, dang mosquito bit my neck. Surprised these bloodthirsty bastards haven't sucked me dry yet," Bill mumbled. "Surprisingly, my blood doth not cause 'em to explode." Samuel couldn't help but smile. Peter caught the contagion as well and smiled.

Peter waved with his hand. "Good day, thee. I have more visits to make. Remember to sow the right seeds and you'll be alright."

"Nice you can see ye think my predicament is humorous," Bill spoke. "Well, I suppose better to laugh than be miserable." He wiped the perspiration from his brow, took off his salt-stained hat, and fanned himself with it. "Speaking of miserable, I hope ye don't wake us up anymore with ye dreaming. Should thee want anyone to talk to? I be here for ye. I don't grant much good advice but I can listen well enough."

Samuel's eyes crinkled with thought. "I know you do, Bill. I know."

"I overheard a little of your words with the general." Bill cleared his throat. "Thou may have lost a brother but ye aye hast me. A crackpot brother, yet a brother nonetheless. Ye hast a whole family of crackpots at thy disposal. Crackpots that will bleed with ye and whip the British."

"You speak the truth, Bill. We are a nation of crackpots yet tis our country, and woe to those that try to take it from us."

CHAPTER 25

FIGHT DARKNESS WITH HUMOR

Sunlight fought to spread its light through the thick canopy. The wind did not blow nor a leaf stir, making the heat even more brutal. Samuel led his men and a few volunteers to patrol a quarter-mile circle around the camp. They totaled eighteen soldiers. They could feel their undershirts clinging with dampness. Jackets became a sweating map of perspiration. They searched for British scouts to prevent them from spotting the rebel camp. The patrol did their best to keep quiet among the woodland ground, but with inexperience, the crunch of twigs and dry leaves could not be prevented. Ever since a large number of the Oneida warriors departed they had been short of adept scouts. If nobody tripped and fell Samuel would consider it a successful mission.

Samuel's muscles that had been fine at the beginning of the patrol now ached. His musket in the ready position gave muscle spasms from his already weak shoulder. This was not the sort of place nor the time of day that Samuel wanted for his injury. The wound was healed now but he still received phantom pain. A strange rustling sound. He forgot the pain. He switched his weapon to the arm of his non-injured side. Suddenly he heard a strange sound. A deep thicket of the brush was shaking at the front of the patrol. "Take cover and prepare to return fire," he whispered. The patrol scrambled to find cover. Samuel cocked his pistol and aimed it at the brush. His eyes did not blink.

A wild turkey appeared from out of the vegetation with not a care in the world. The turkey's head was so ugly it appeared beautiful. Its large black body resembled a giant pheasant. Two more turkeys followed the first with no fear. The gobbling turkeys stopped and Samuel's men stared. It was a showdown. A soldier cocked his firearm. "Delay that," Samuel whispered loudly. "Do you want to give away our positions to the British?"

A few sighs were heard and a mumble from someone unknown, "Dang 'd be tasty, sergeant."

"Besides the noise, I like 'em. They seem silly birds but I applaud their courage."

Samuel felt his dry mouth with his tongue. "No turkey today, but you can have some water. Drink some now and that's not a request." Out came wooden canteens with warm water. Although the water was warm and tasted horrible it was nonetheless refreshing.

Other than an opportunity to destroy a determined force of turkeys they found no threats on the patrol. The patrol headed back to camp to report and swap for a fresh group to continue patrolling and scouting.

Cato leaned on a spruce tree next to Samuel's tent, a blade of grass between his teeth.

"Cato Bannister, glad to see you. Here tell you were looking for me earlier," bellowed Samuel.

"My pardon, sergeant, doth you have time for a private moment."

Although exhausted from the patrol, Samuel covered the strain with a smile. "For a friend from back home, you bet. Shall we walk?"

The men strolled together, keeping to the outskirts of the camp. Cato turned to Samuel, his skin glistening at the nape of his neck.

"The Rhode Island militia knows your brother to be departed. I would like to grant my condolences and those of my unit for your loss. Duncan was a good lad."

Samuel received a chill through his bones despite a bead of sweat rolling off his forehead down his nose. He took off his hat, fanned himself, and scrubbed his hands through his hair. "Thank you, Cato, this means a lot to me. The loss of Duncan has been hard to bear. I often ponder how the memories of those souls that have sacrificed for freedom shall be recalled, especially would we lose this war." Samuel began to rub his aching shoulder, out of habit. "The last battle we fought was really a good retreat. The British are persistent. Think of Breed's Hill; they were decimated at point-blank range and still, they advanced."

Cato looked sullen. "I believe we will win. Revolution has spread like the pox. We are protecting home and kin. The British fight for a king and a tyrant. Too, they traveled a vast distance to dispatch their own brothers. What kind of motivation can their soldiers truly hast?"

Samuel scoffed. "Their own brothers? Maybe some, but we are a melting pot of many who have escaped their countries for a better life than suffer the rules of their government. You ask me, their soldiers are more likely to lose motivation seeing freedom and wanting it for themselves." Samuel paused as he wiped his forehead. "Any in your regiment hear news about Newport?"

"Newport is still under siege. General John Sullivan is in command of our forces there. He's a tough one if y' bid me."

"I believe you. I served under that tough-as-nails Irishman."

"I hear that there is talk with French support that Newport may finally break the yoke of the British, perhaps as soon as August. Don't wot would I trust the French."

"If Washington does that's enough for me. With their aid, we can really take it to 'em and recapture Newport. I hate knowing my parents are under 'em. I can't imagine what those poor people hast suffered through."

Suddenly, a large man dressed as militia, with a beige jacket with blue cuffs and collar and sand-colored breaches, thumped into Cato. Cato knocked off balance, stumbled, and nearly fell. The militiaman who seemed oddly chubby for a soldier kept walking as if nothing happened. Samuel's eyes narrowed to slits. His face reddened and he was about to unleash a volley of obscenities. Cato, sensing Samuel about to explode, waved him off. Cato forced a fake smile. "I take no offense enough to start a fight, bet he was probably just from one of those southern colonies. They're more terrified of a slave revolt than fighting the British. Southern militias were founded for that reason. Even Washington did not want us initially in his army until the British offered slaves an opportunity to earn their freedom. We have since proved our worth and Washington is a believer now. We makeup thousands of the army now, maybe even as much as one out of every five men. We are integrated as brothers and not i' separate units."

"It's still not right," Samuel grumbled.

"No, not right, but not your battle to fight. Please let it pass."

Samuel rubbed his neck while he continued to walk.

"Samuel, you may have lost Duncan but you have many a bother here and even after the war the bonds of brotherhood will not be shed. Well, maybe not the ass that knocked into me. He ain't worth keeping. He would rail till his legs broke beneath him would he have to shed a few pounds. They say an army runs on food; this guy must have a key to supply. Blessed are those who hunger and thirst, for they are being devoted to their diet." Cato smiled on the edge of bursting. The dam burst as they laughed till their bellies ached. Bystanders' attention was caught and they wanted to share in the pun, but it was a private moment.

The laughter made their steps feel lighter. It had been a long time since either laughed out loud. Laughter is a light to fight away the darkness. It can replace stress, anxiety, anguish, fear, and grief in our hearts. It can even resist the shadow of death but that will not stop it from coming.

CHAPTER 26

TIDES OF CHANGE

The exhausted, mosquito-bitten, Continental army struggled on in the humid, stifling air. For days, the temperature stood well above 90 degrees. Violent evening thunderstorms turned the dusty roads to sludge. Samuel and his brigade found themselves with the force Washington commanded. Washington gave orders to break camp and abandon all heavy baggage to push for speed in pursuit of the British. The exhausted pursuit went into the night and ended in the morning.

On the morning of June 28th, Samuel rested against a tree and hastily gulped the last of his breakfast, bread, and cheese, and brushed a few crumbs from his waistcoat.

Bill nudged Samuel with his finger. "We were scattered like sheep all night. It's actually amazing we could find each other in the morning."

"Well, at least we hast a good shepherd among us."

"Hey, I quoth I raised 'em on my farm, but it's not my primary occupation.

"Shepherd or not, you have a good eye."

"At least the British didn't have a good eye; they could have advanced on us in the confusion."

"Nah, they're moving as fast as they can move their ass. Will catch 'em, though. Lee is on their tail."

Samuel frowned. "Don't care much for Lee. 'Tis heard he was originally offered command, yet declined believing the force wasn't large enough for his taste. So Washington granted it to Lafayette with Hamilton to assist. Wherein the force grew to 6,000, almost half the size of Washington's entire army. It finally dawned on him to replace Lafayette. What could Washington doth? Lee has more experience than Lafayette."

"I heard he calls Lafayette 'La petite French boy.'"

The roar of drums signaled the men to dress ranks and prepare for battle. Samuel snatched up his coat and musket quickly. The men formed ranks then stood in position with time the only rank marching on. The lucky ones were in the shade although it did not make a great difference. They suffered in the heat, faces sagging with weariness and worry. It did not take long for a few to fall out of formation. Samuel took off his tricorn hat and did his best to fan himself and kept an eye on his men. They held in position for what seemed an eternity.

You could feel it whispered in the wind. The tides of time were about to shift. A pivotal moment for the floundering revolution was about to occur. The rebels would either change the tide to a much-needed victory or sink further in quagmire, unable to crawl their way back. Patriot leaders' dreams of freedom would be realized, otherwise, they'd hang for sure. The stakes were huge.

King George III had recently replaced General Howe for General Henry Clinton to command the British campaign. During the 1777 campaign season, the British failed to deal the Rebel Army a mortal blow by splitting the colonies in half. The British campaign in 1778 would take a different approach; they would rely more on offenses that took advantage of their mighty sea power and aid from loyalist sentiment, still a large part of the population.

Clinton's intention, in accordance with his orders, was to march north and fortify New York after the French agreed to support the Americans. The first week of marching convinced Clinton that his army with its long support train would never make the journey by land. In addition, it was reported that Revolutionary General Gates was moving from the Hudson River valley with his forces to block the British retreat. Clinton decided to divert to the coast and take ships. At Allentown, his army branched off the main route towards Monmouth.

On June 18th word came to rebels that the British army was on the move after they abandoned Philadelphia. After confirming this was true Washington followed the slow-moving British column looking to strike a lethal blow. Washington sent approximately one-third of his force ahead under the command of Major General Charles Lee, hoping that Lee would strike the British flank without entering into a major engagement. Washington with the main Army would then attack Clinton's army in the rear to finish them. For the first time, Washington had sufficient numbers and confidence to land a knockout blow. This was the opportunity he had been praying for on behalf of the Revolution; only no battle ever went according to plan, even the best. The greatness was finding victory after those plans began to fall apart.

At around 1 p.m. distant gunfire was heard. A few shots at first, then a peppering sound of a large engagement. The ranks broke to let in a rider who immediately reported to Washington. Although the rider clutched his shoulder with blood seeping out he held a look of confidence. "General, dispatch from Lee. He wants you to know he is encircling the enemy. We will win the day."

Washington's face beamed with confidence and delight. "Go to the rear and see to your wound." He turned to Hamilton. "That arrogant man is gonna do it. I'll give "em all the fame that he doth lack if he wins the day. Let's stick to the plan and move forward along Monmouth road."

"Yes, General."

Washington should have gone with his gut. Lee acted poorly in his command giving poor orders to his officers. He simply allowed them to engage the enemy as they saw fit. Skirmishes with parties of British troops took place, as Lee's force somehow managed to move forward towards Middletown Road. A cluster of fighting broke out against a disciplined British rear guard. Lee's force was not up to the task and he ordered a retreat to the main army under Washington. As Lee retreated down the road, Clinton launched an all-out pursuit. In his mind, the Americans would be easier to defeat than he thought.

Just under an hour, a terrified adolescent fifer came down the road, running, mumbling of disaster. "Flee, you fools! Save yourselves! The redcoats have taken the field, they smashed through the lines. It's butchery." The fifer maneuvered through the main force until an officer grabbed him by his scruff and shook the information out of him. His story was soon confirmed by a few soldiers slogging down the road, then hundreds, some collapsing from the murderous heat as they made their way to safety.

An astonished Washington could not figure out why they were retreating. He questioned every officer he could find but found no coherent answer. At last, down the road, Charles Lee came riding, covered in dust. Washington, face red with rage and his white-knuckled hand clutching his saber, confronted Lee. "You, sir, are retreating in considerable disorder, with the British advancing behind you. What the &#%!, &#%!" Washington unleashed a volley of cuss words at Lee, to the astonishment of those listening, before ordering Lee to the rear. Washington then kicked his horse, galloping forward, then began the difficult task of rallying Lee's disordered troops and forming them into his force before the British assault.

"Well, we didn't get all dressed up for nutin," Bill explained.

"Do you take anything seriously?" said Samuel.

"I'm as serious as the friggin' pox when it comes to killing me some redcoats. That you can mark.

"Consider it so."

"Ye here that?

> *Yankee Doodle came to town*
> *For to buy a firelock:*
> *We will tar and feather him*
> *And so we will John Hancock.*

"At a walk!" Washington shouted, to be heard as loud as possible. All along the line, other voices echoed him. "Advance!"

Just as the order was given the British in full bayonet charge encountered Washington's army. They slowed and tried desperately to dress ranks with the rebels. British officers shouted on horseback, pointing with their sabers, but they were not able to form quickly enough. Washington's army was in tight ranks, prepared to unleash a hail of musket balls. Washington was surrounded by his personal guard, waving their white silk flag that depicted a guard holding a horse's reins and a woman personified as Liberty leaning upon the Union shield, near an American eagle. The rebel officers in the front ranks watched the flood of British come into view charging. They hastily called out to their troops, shouting, "Make ready!" The order was passed along from officers to sergeants: "Make ready!" Then a loud command from Washington: "Fire!"

Samuel was in position just behind the first American line. The front line fired then knelt down to reload as the second line discharged their muskets. The British, still in a bayonet charge, haphazardly moved to form into battle lines. It was a scene of carnage as the British were cut down from the heavy fire. The British attempted to return fire but it was of little use until they could form. The Rebels, a force they saw fleeing moments ago, were moving with disciplined precision. The men who had suffered so much at Valley Forge were now taking hurt to the British. The armies slugged it out with loud cracks of gunfire.

A thundering boom sounded as Washington's cannons were able to direct fire onto the British position and unleash hell. Heavy cannonballs bounced off the ground tearing men apart. The smoke from the cannon fire impaired the men's vision as they loaded and fired as quickly as possible. Washington with his guard surrounding him moved through the grey cloud yelling, "Fire at will! Fire at will! Take it to 'em for liberty!"

Samuel dropped to one knee taking careful aim at a British officer who was pointing with a saber, attempting to assemble a cluster of men. Samuel pulled the hammer back on his musket then squeezed the trigger. A sharp crack of fire rang out with a puff of grey smoke. The officer was struck in the chest and went down. Without warning a loud ringing sound in Samuel's ear—a soldier had let loose a shot from his musket just above Samuel's body close to his ear. Samuel's ears rang as he fought off his temporary deafness. The soldier that fired moved forward, oblivious to the incident. Samuel froze for a few heartbeats holding both ears.

From the corner of his eye, Samuel saw the union flag bearer take a hail of shots and slump to the ground. He waved and hollered till he received the attention of a brigade officer directly in front of him. Samuel pointed to the torn and tattered continental colors lying on the ground. The officer shook his head but took no immediate action. A sudden urge struck Samuel like a hammer to his head to grab the flag and rescue it safely to the American lines. He was not the only one. He watched as fearless men charged desperately to recover the flag. All the brave souls were cut down quickly by murderous fire. British soldiers feverishly wanted to capture the flag for themselves and they began to shift and spread out in preparations to make an attempt. If captured, the flag, with its 13 horizontal alternating red and white stripes, would give them a great sense of pride subsequently bringing dishonor to the rebels. Volleys of shots went back and forth between the rebels and British creating a fog of heavy grey and black smoke.

Samuel checked the men surrounding him. If an officer shall not take charge I will. Too many have sacrificed for that flag. "You see that flag!" he yelled. "To let it fall in enemy hands would be like leaving a brother behind!" He tapped about a dozen to lay down suppressing fire directly in front of the flag. This time it was the British that pursued the flag under massed accurate fire. They were relentless in their hunt of the flag. British officers shouted and pointed towards the flag pressing men to their deaths. One redcoat crawled slowly on his hands and knees thinking he could sneak up and grab the flag. He was met with a red spray to his head. The Americans tried again to take the flag and so did the British. Valiant attempts were made on both sides to take the prize with no efforts succeeding. The only prize received was blood.

After hearing the drum roll call of retreat, it would be the British turn this time to feel the sting of defeat, bested by ragtag revolutionaries made up of Continentals and militia. The British relinquished the field and the stalemate ended. The beacon for union and liberty remained crumpled on the ground. With a motion, Samuel pointed to the flag and hollered, "Charge!" He then ran as fast as his legs would carry him towards the flag. His men directly under his command followed closely behind him. Samuel grabbed the flag and waved it with abandon. "You try and take our liberty, we shall bring you death! Huzzah! Huzzah!" After the final "Huzzah" Samuel felt a sudden pain. Something ran down his face and dripped in front of his eye. Blood. With a groan, he collapsed just before passing the flag to the closest man near him, William Anthony, aka Bill.

"Sniper!" screamed Bill. Men surrounded Samuel to offer help. Samuel fought to keep conscious. He listened as the sound of sporadic fire faded as the entire army pressed forward and pursued the British. Samuel was gently moved to a grassy spot a few feet from where he fell. Waives of pain contorted his face. In the grip of soundless panic, heart racing, rising blood pressure, his eyes welled with tears. This is the end. I'm going to die, Mother. He heard a gentle voice.

"Don't move, I have you." He recognized the voice as Molly Hays, aka Molly Pitcher, from his hospital visit. "I have him."

"Mo— Mo— Molly, how did you get to the front?" Samuel whimpered in pain.

Molly turned to the men that had laid Samuel down. "Now off with you boys, they'll be needing that flag to raise spirits. I promise he will be in good charge." The men promptly returned to the fight and joined the army in pursuit of the British. Bill continued holding the flag and waved his way to the front ranks. His display rallied and energized every witness. Samuel could hear Bill shouting "Liberty!" until the voice faded with the distance.

Molly wiped the blood from his wounded eye with a rag. "I was sponging out the guns between shots when my husband's cannon took casualties." She smiled "Methought I would lend a hand and fire some shots. I helped shoot the cannon till the order was given to hold so not to fire upon our own men. I presently ran to help the wounded, then mine eye caught the broil scene of the flag unfolds."

Samuel listened till he passed out. A litter carried him to be treated at the rear in a "flying" makeshift hospital tent.

The battle of Monmouth was over and would quickly grow into a legend. The victory was actually more of a draw for the Continental forces since Washington's army had won the battle and the British managed to escape with most of their long supply chain intact but it was a turning point for the war. The Americans held the field against one of the greatest military forces on earth. Finally, Washington had his victory he could build on.

Samuel heard good news filled with bad news. The good news: He would keep his eye. The bad news: Along with a large scar that would permanently mark his face, one eye had been damaged severely and he would never see out of it again. He was offered the choice to continue his service or be released back home. None would ever say he had not done his part to sacrifice in the revolution. Should he continue in service to the cause of liberty or return home to his family? It was like two people battling out in his head. One said, "Do not abandon your comrades and brothers, the war is not won yet." The other said, "Do not abandon your parents, you're their only remaining child, who will help them when they get old." In deep reflection, he toiled with his thoughts. There were two families to choose from. He compromised his feelings by remaining in the army in a non-combat role. He would be accepted as an aide to Washington.

Leaving the hospital tent, a cool breeze came in unexpectedly as he went to sit by a large oak tree. Hamilton was there with Lafayette, resting against the tree. They were in a pitiful state of exhaustion. Hamilton and Lafayette had been close to Washington on the battle line as he directed the battle. They were ceaseless in their efforts, charging, and rallying the men. Hamilton motioned for Samuel to lay beside the tree with them. He took off a blanket he had wrapped around himself and insisted Samuel take it. Samuel wrapped himself and drifted to sleep.

Alone on the battlefield, Washington walked amid the carnage. He remained until all the dead and wounded were collected. The victory gave his heart great joy, but also deep sorrow for those that lost their lives under his command. The dead never complain but he would not fail them because of their sacrifices. He would never give up the fight for liberty. A new nation would be established and represented by the Citizens of an American Nation.

Washington walked off the battlefield and beneath the old oak tree found Hamilton and Lafayette, next to them a wounded Samuel with a bloody bandage around his head that covered one eye. A gentle breeze stirred the tree. Washington closed his eyes for a moment and breathed in the air. Taking off his dusty coat he shook it off then gently placed it over Hamilton and Lafayette. More work needed to be done, more blood and sacrifice, but for now a moment of peace. He sat down alongside the tree, took off his hat, and stretched out. He could feel the tiredness inside and his eyes glazed over. He nodded off with a smile across his face.

EPILOGUE

This nation owes a great deal of gratitude to the patriots of the American Revolution that may not include who you think. We need to keep in our memories the truth of who fought for the cause of Independence, which included the often overlooked Native Americans and African Americans, who made great sacrifices for the cause. A great integrated coalition helped bring us to victory over the British, a superpower at the time, as well as deep Christian roots that were strongly planted.

We were given a false vision in school that civilian farmers picked up their rifles above the mantelpiece and fought for the cause of liberty. In truth, a majority of the men were drawn from the dispossessed classes of society with little if any marketable skill or property. These men were willing to take poor pay, often deferred, harsh discipline, sometimes rotten food, and often insufficient shelter and clothing. Of the patriots in the Revolution, more than 30,000 died, 8,000 as prisoners, 17,000 of diseases in the camp, and 6,800 in battle. Nearly 1,500 disappeared and 8,000 would be maimed for life. Nearly 1,500 disappeared and 8,000 would be maimed for life. The Union Army in the Civil War had a casualty rate of just over 10 percent casualties—that is, those killed, wounded, or missing in action. In the American Revolution nearly 20 percent of all soldiers who served turned out to be a casualty. The rate was higher among the regulars of the Continental Army, nearly 1 out of 3 versus the militia.

We also owe a debt to the Native Americans for their sacrifice of blood and provisions during the Revolution as well as for helping teach us democracy and women's rights. Although most of the Native Americans chose the British, many chose not to abandon us. Among these were included large numbers from the Oneidas, Tuscaroras, Mohicans, and the Stockbridge Nations. Hundreds of American Indians enlisted in the Continental Army, such as the Stockbridge and Mohican Indians, which were part of several New England regiments in Connecticut and Massachusetts. Many other American Indians served as scouts in specialized units. Ten Oneida soldiers would later attain officers' commissions in the Continental Army, and one rose to the rank of lieutenant-colonel. Washington and his wife Martha would never forget Polly for her generosity. She was offered pay, but she refused any because she said it was her duty to serve her country. As a gift of appreciation, Martha would later bring Polly to Philadelphia and buy her a bonnet, hat, and shawl. Many great speeches were made later acknowledging the Native American contribution and Congress did set aside six million acres for the Oneida in 1788, but today all that remains after many broken promises is a pathetic 32 acres. The Haudenosaunee Confederation or Alliance was among six tribal nations. The Great Law of Peace given by this Alliance is one of the nearest examples of democracy of which the founding fathers took notice. Confederation Tribes were pro-women's rights. The tribes were ruled by women with clan ties traced through descent.

Although history would forget their brave stand, African Americans served as a large source for the Continental Army. Many fought for American freedom, although they themselves had none. Early in the early days of the Revolution, many African Americans from the New England states enlisted. It's been said that the American Army during the Revolution was the most racially integrated it would be until the Korean War. Nearly 5,000 fought as free men and slaves. Many more filled such important roles as laborers. It is estimated that up to 25% of the American Army at the final battle of Yorktown for American Independence was African American.

Finally, history forgets the groundswell of faith and prayer during the fight for a new nation. Many Americans have forgotten or choose to ignore the Christian roots of our nation's founding. It is important that we do not forget it, for doing so ignores our heritage and the sacrifices made to found our nation. Though America was not a theocracy, its Founding was deeply shaped by Christianity. Many historic documents and speeches exist that prove the founders' Christian roots. In one of the earliest acts of Congress on September 11th, 1777, before Congress was forced to flee Philadelphia, during a desperate time in the American Revolution, they voted to order twenty thousand Bibles. As was written in the Journals of Continental Congress, "The use of the Bible is so universal, and its importance so great."

George Washington survived a war despite having a number of horses shot out from under him, narrowly escaping bullets and cannonball blasts. Was this due to divine intervention? Washington was rumored to have prayed on his hands and knees in the darkest hours of Valley Forge. The war at that time was not going well. The men were starving; they did not know if certain European allies would help them. There was even a plot to replace Washington with a different commander to lead the Revolution. Whether he prayed like this or not, miracles abounded at Valley Forge. The American army was trained, needed supplies and reinforcements arrived, and France joined the American War for Independence. This was the moment God chose to deliver the Americans from the yoke of the British.

Washington never liked to publicly show his own faith, but when he chose to, his religious rhetoric was earnest and heartfelt. Frequently in his writings and speeches, he would add the words "Blessings of Heaven and Providence." When he presented his military resignation at the end of the Revolutionary war with deep emotion, he declared it was the power of the Union and the protection of Almighty God that got the army through the war. Early in his presidency, at the request of Congress, he issued the first National Thanksgiving Proclamation on October 3, 1789. It urged the people in the young country to express their gratitude to God for his protection of them through the Revolutionary War and the peace they had experienced since. The proclamation also stated that "It is the duty of all nations to acknowledge the providence of Almighty God, to obey His will, to be grateful for His benefits."

Samuel Adams was a signer of the Declaration of Independence, ratifier of our Constitution, and Governor of Massachusetts. He was a man of liberty, who had endured misfortunes that would have broken an ordinary man. His wife and four of his children died before the war began. At Bunker Hill, the British beheaded Adam's dear friend Joseph Warren and displayed it as a trophy. The vengeful British vandalized his home, making it uninhabitable. If the revolution failed it may have been his head presented as a trophy.

Adams believed God was intervening on the side of the Colonists. He compared the Colonies breaking away from Britain to the Israelites that had left the bondage of slavery in Egypt. In a fast day proclamation, he proclaimed, "I conceive we cannot better express ourselves than by humbly supplicating the Supreme Ruler of the world . . . that the confusions that are and have been among the nations may be overruled by the promoting and speedily bringing in the holy and happy period when the kingdoms of our Lord and Savior Jesus Christ may be everywhere established, and the people willingly bow to the scepter of Him who is the Prince of Peace."

Adams was a steadfast Christian to the end and publicly displayed it. During my research, I found many false references to his last will and testament, which can be found in the New York County Probate Records, Volume Eight (1705-53).

Many quote his last will and testament as stating the following: "Principally and first of all I Give and Recommend my soul into the Hands of God that gave it, hoping thro' the Merits, death, and

Passion of my savior Jesus Christ, to have full and free pardon and forgiveness of all my Sins and to Enherit Eternal life." This is in fact from his son John Quincy Adams' last will and testament, according to the Papers of John Adams, volume 1, Massachusetts Historical Society, Digital Edition.

I have used Washington and Adams, as two incredible authors of our country, to show Christian roots in the establishment of our nation. Naysayers would state America's Founders were guided by atheist beliefs, class, or state interests. They don't deny that the Founders were strict, yet they contend that they were for the most part deists, people who reject numerous Christian principles, and who figure God doesn't meddle in the undertakings of men and countries.

Based on the Founders' own words and writings, I contend that not only did America have Christian roots in our founding, but virtually all of the Founders were devout Christians who believed political and religious goals were fundamentally intertwined. We cannot ignore the truth that our nation's Founders believed that democracy required liberty but also faith.

---

[2]From a Fast Day Proclamation issued by Governor Samuel Adams, Massachusetts, March 20, 1797, in our possession; see also Samuel Adams, The Writings of Samuel Adams, Harry Alonzo Cushing, editor (New York: G. P. Putnam's Sons, 1908), Vol. IV, p. 407, from his proclamation of March 20, 1797

SOURCES

"Just the Essentials: Clothing and Equipment of Revolutionary War Soldiers." Minute Man National Historical Park. National Park Service, U. S. Department of the Interior. 2009. https://www.nps.gov/mima/forteachers/upload/essentials.pdf (accessed February 25, 2013).

Bilharz, Joy "Oriskany: A place of Great Sadness" A Mohawk Battlefield Ethnography, Northeast Region Ethnography Program National Park Service, Boston, MA 2009.

Bloomfield, J,K. "The Oneidas",Alden Brothers, New York, 1907.

Glatthaar, Joseph T., and James Kirby Martin. Forgotten Allies: The Oneida Indians and the American Revolution. New York: Hill and Wang, 2006. Print.

Graymont, Barbara. The Iroquois in the American Revolution. Syracuse University Press, 1972. Print.

Jackson, John W. Valley Forge: Pinnacle of Courage. Gettysburg: Thomas Publications, 1992. Print.

Levinson, David. "An Explanation For The Oneida-Colonial Alliance In The American Revolution." Ethnohistory 1976. Print.

Reed, John. "Barren Hill." Valley Forge Journal. Print.

Also from this author:

THE FAITH
OF A CENTURION

Available at Amazon
and Barnes & Noble.

CPSIA information can be obtained
at www.ICGtesting.com
Printed in the USA
LVHW080428020721
691545LV00016BA/1320